© 2005 by YouthLight, Inc.
Chapin, SC 29036

All rights reserved. Permission is given for individuals to reproduce the activities and worksheet section in this book. Reproduction of any other material is strictly prohibited.

Illustrated by David Bass • Cover Design and Layout by Diane Florence • Project Editing by Susan Bowman

ISBN
1-889636-82-7

Library of Congress Number
2004115156

10 9 8 7 6 5 4 3 2 1
Printed in the United States

★ DEDICATION

This Program is being dedicated to my dear and loving mother, Mrs. Shirley Jean Chanaca. Thank you for all your love and support throughout my life. You have been the inspiration for winning and persevering in life for all of your family for so many years. Your indomitable spirit and zest for life and learning has been contagious to everyone who has come in contact with your life and has been realized in the goals that you set for yourself: wife, mother, nurse, counselor, world traveler, and even Black Belt at 65 years of age! As you prepared us for school assignments; plays, athletic events, speeches, and travel opportunities, you set our minds to enjoy all that life had to offer. You instilled in us an awe of God and all that He has created. You have been a life-long learner who still gets excited about a sunset. You have passed this passion down to those whom you love. Most of the concepts that are in the Super Student Program came from the training that you instilled in your children so long ago. All of these ideas needed to be written down so others could be helped along the way. God has blessed you with the ability to foster and promote attainable dreams for those whom you love and whose lives you touch. You have helped us develop positive and healthy attitudes. In addition, you have taught us that we have a choice every-day regarding the attitude we will embrace for that day. Thank you, Mother. I can never repay you. You have fulfilled the quote in Proverbs 31:28, "Her children rise up and call her blessed." You have inspired us to reach for the stars in all that we do. In so doing, this program is a gift from you.

Attitude

" The longer I live, the more I realize the impact of attitude on life.
Attitude to me is more important than facts.
It is more important than past, than education, than money,
Than circumstances, than failure, than successes,
Than what other people think say or do.

It is more important than appearance, giftedness or skill.
It will make or break a company…a church …a school … a home …a person.

The remarkable thing is we have a choice every day
Regarding the attitude we will embrace for that day.
We cannot change our past….
We cannot change the fact that people will act in a certain way.
We cannot change the inevitable.
The only thing we can do is play on the one string we have, and it is our attitude..
I am convinced that life is 10% what happens to me
And 90% how I react to it. And so it is with you…
We are in charge of our attitudes."

– Charles Swindoll

TABLE OF CONTENTS

Dedication 2
Acknowledgements 6
Overview 7
Introduction 9
Rationale 12
Elements of the Super Student Program 14
   • Objective 14
   • Four Parts of the Program 14
      1. Stories and Lessons 14
      2. The Super Student Club and Awards Celebration 15
      3. The Survival Kit for the Teacher 17
      4. The Survival Kit for the Parent 17
Questions and Answers for the Professional Educator 18
Adapting the Super Student Program for Small Groups and Individual Help 25

★ **The *Super Student Program* for Grades K-1** 26

The Key Maker 28
   • Lesson 1   Talon's Problem 29
       Activity 1.1 31
       Activity 1.2 31
   • Lesson 2   The Club 32
       Activity 1.3 35
   • Lesson 3   Meeting the Old Man 36
       Activity 1.4 40
       Activity 1.5 40
   • Lesson 4   The White Key 41
       Activity 1.6 43
       Activity 1.7 43
   • Lesson 5   The Yellow Key 44
       Activity 1.8 46
       Activity 1.9 46
   • Lesson 6   The Green Key 47
       Activity 1.10 49
       Activity 1.11 49
   • Lesson 7   The Red Key 50
       Activity 1.12 52
       Activity 1.13 52
   • Lesson 8   The Blue Key 53
       Activity 1.14 56
       Activity 1.15 56
   • Lesson 9   The Black Key 57

© Youthlight, Inc.

TABLE OF CONTENTS

    Activity 1.16 59
    Activity 1.17 59
 • Lesson 10 The Pledge 60

The Super Student Club Packet 64
Black line Masters for Grades K-1 65

★ The *Super Student Program* for Grades for Grades 2-3 75

Talon and the Magic Eggs 77
 • Lesson 1 The Project 78
    Activity 2.1 81
 • Lesson 2 Meeting Talon 82
    Activity 2.2 86
    Activity 2.3 86
 • Lesson 3 The White Egg 87
    Activity 2.4 89
 • Lesson 4 The Yellow Egg 90
    Activity 2.5 92
    Activity 2.6 92
 • Lesson 5 The Orange Egg 93
    Activity 2.7 97
 • Lesson 6 The Green Egg 98
    Activity 2.8 100
    Activity 2.9 100
    Activity 2.10 101
 • Lesson 7 The Brown Egg 102
 • Lesson 8 The Red Egg 105
    Activity 2.11 107
 • Lesson 9 The Blue Egg 108
 • Lesson 10 The Black Egg 112
    Activity 2.12 117
    Activity 2.13 117

The Super Student Club Packet 119
Black line Masters for Grades 2-3 120

★ The *Super Student Program* for Grades 4-5 146

The Old Man 147
 • Lesson 1 The Storm 148
    Activity 3.1 155

TABLE OF CONTENTS

- Lesson 2 The Survival Kit 156
    - Activity 3.2 163
    - Activity 3.3 163
- Lesson 3 The White Seal 164
    - Activity 3.4 167
    - Activity 3.5 167
- Lesson 4 The Yellow Seal 168
    - Activity 3.6 172
    - Activity 3.7 172
- Lesson 5 The Orange Seal 173
    - Activity 3.8 178
- Lesson 6 The Green Seal 179
    - Activity 3.9 181
- Lesson 7 The Brown Seal 182
    - Activity 3.10 184
- Lesson 8 The Red Seal...185
    - Activity 3.11 188
- Lesson 9 The Blue Seal 189
    - Activity 3.12 194
    - Activity 3.13 194
- Lesson 10 The Black Seal 195
    - Activity 3.14 203
    - Activity 3.15 203
    - Activity 3.16 203
    - Activity 3.17 204

The Super Student Packet 205
Black line Masters for Grades 4-5 206

A Survival Kit for the Teacher: the Master Chef 242
The Magic Eight for Teachers...243
A Survival Kit for Parents 249
The Magic Eight for Parents...251

About The Author 258
References 259

★ ACKNOWLEDGEMENTS

The development of the *Super Student Program* has been a work in progress for over thirty-five years. It represents the experiences that I have had in the public school system with children in elementary school. I especially wish to acknowledge the following:

★ My dear and lovely wife, Jane who listened, read, reviewed and offered many suggestions throughout this program and previous publications. Thank you Jane, for your love and support throughout our many years of marriage.

★ Our children, Mark and Joel, both were the inspiration for the characters in the stories that formed the *Super Student* concepts. Both of you were gifts from God to your mother and me.

★ Mr. and Mrs. John Chanaca, Sr., for continual, encouragement and love that instilled a winning attitude in me.

★ Ms. Cheryl Gredlein, my niece, who proofread the program and gave me encouragement all during the process.

★ David and Dawn Chanaca, my brother and sister-in-law, who listened one Thanksgiving afternoon to the ramblings of an educator set to make a difference.

★ The Stroudsburg School District in Pennsylvania and the Horry County School District in South Carolina for allowing me to work with their children for over thirty-five years.

★ Mrs. Shirley Huggins, Principal and the staff and students of Green Sea Floyds Elementary School, Green Sea, South Carolina, who provided the freedom and opportunity to develop the *Super Student* concepts.

★ Mrs. Sherry Quick, curriculum coordinator, and Mrs. Bebe Harrelson, Asst. Principal who guided and promoted the *Super Student Program* at Green Sea.

★ Mrs. Deborah Gants, friend and educator who proofed and gave story suggestions for the Program.

★ Dr. Bob Bowman and his lovely wife, Susan have been mentors and friends as well as publishers of this work.

★ Dr. Muriel O'Tuel, who first saw the potential of the *Super Student* concepts in the *Peer Pals Program* and encouraged me to continue to write my ideas down.

★ Mrs. Dorothy Dietrick, my first cooperating teacher and dear friend over the last thirty-five years. I thank God for bringing you and your husband, Norman into my life.

★ To all my teachers from elementary school through graduate school, I say thank you. The Lord has blessed me through you. You have made a difference.

★ OVERVIEW

The *Super Student Program* is a program designed to improve student achievement and behavior. The Program challenges students to be personally responsible for their learning by giving them the survival tools necessary to win in school. It encourages students to choose to be winners in school.

For your students, basic Super Student Focus Skills are introduced through three engaging and interactive stories. Each story is designed for a particular grade level and is beautifully illustrated. Activity sheets accompany each of the skills throughout the stories. Presented in a club format, the students are invited to join the "The Super Student Club" at the end of the story. The committed members are then presented the Super Student Focus Sheet, pledge, membership card and certificate. During the course of each marking period, they are invited to renew their membership and commitment as teachers work with the concepts and skills during community circle time. A celebration program for the Super Students is strongly recommended every marking period to recognize their achievements. The *Super Student Program* gives educators suggestions to form their Super Student Awards Celebration.

The preparation for the Program takes only fifteen to twenty minutes twice a week for five weeks. All of this is done during community circle or shared reading time. The stories are engaging and interesting. At the end of each story/lesson are appropriate questions and activities to further develop your students into Super Students. The stories contain all the work you would normally do during a shared reading time or language arts period with your students. Teachers consider it part of their reading program. So, you are doing academics while you are working with the *Super Student Program*!

However, the *Super Student Program* is flexible. The teacher or counselor could read the stories over a longer time with the class thus developing the club over a longer period of time. In addition, the program has been used with small groups in counseling, follow-up sessions and individual counseling situations with excellent results. Special education classes and resource room students benefit dramatically from the skills and worksheet activities. This Program has also been very successful in developing behavioral intervention plans (BIP) for special education students. Regular education students who need behavior plans have also benefited.

The Program also contains a teacher and parent section.

For the teacher, a section called "A Survival Kit for the Teacher" introduces eight steps to develop Super Students in the classroom. Helpful hints and techniques to be a master teacher and developer of Super Students are included.

For the parent, it invites parents to be partners with the school in raising a Super Student. Helpful hints for parents are included in the Program in a section entitled "A Survival Kit for the Parents." Parents are also invited to help their children memorize the Super Student Focus Skills and My Pledge.

The *Super Student Program* is researched based and built on basic truths about learning. It highly values student choice, along with reverence for teaching and learning. It acknowledges obedience growing from respect. It encourages and promotes effort from students. It believes in positive recognition based on achieved personal educational goals. It is positive and encouraging. It believes in possibilities and student potential. Finally, it is passionate about achievement.

I believe that any student can become a Super Student. It is all about a super attitude! A Super Student has a positive attitude about the possibilities of school and learning. This Program will help develop that positive attitude. A Super Student is respectful and responsible. This student is always

© Youthlight, Inc.

★ OVERVIEW (CONTINUED)

giving his/her best, trusting the teacher to lead the way. He/she is always pushing himself/herself further. This student is a self-disciplined life-long learner. Sound impossible? The good news is that this student is made not born. Achievement is a natural bi-product of this super attitude.

Super Students are winning in school and have learned the skills that make good things happen to them. They believe in themselves. They are persistent. In short, they have learned how to be successful and happy in school. They have learned how to focus on forming certain habits that continue to cause them to win in school. Good grades, good behavior, and high achievement test scores are the result of this kind of attitude. Most of all, the warm feeling of having done one's best is evident. Super Students are happy to come to school to be nurtured and they will use the skills they learn throughout their life.

The Super Student Program has highlighted the skills required to be successful in today's global educational community.

THE SUPER STUDENT FOCUS SKILLS ARE:

1. I will listen, obey, and trust my teacher.
2. I will raise my hand to speak.
3. I will think along with the speaker.
4. I will be prepared for my work.
5. I will give my best.
6. I will finish all my work.
7. I will work out problems with others.
8. I will have a positive, healthy attitude.

My Pledge

My attitude is the only thing I can control in life. I can choose to be happy or sad, helpful or hurtful. I can choose to be a winner in school. My attitude is reflected in these Super Student Focus Skills. I will read these Focus Skills every day. I will practice these skills to show I am a winner. People will see me doing these things, and good things will happen to me! As I focus on these skills, I will feel happy inside. Being GOOD is good for me! I really want to be a winner in school!

★ INTRODUCTION

Schools are in the business of creating successful learners and achievers. Students come to us ready to recognize their special, unique ingredients and ready to be gently coaxed into their future haute cuisine—that of a life-long learner. Somewhere along the line, if the student is fortunate and willing, a parent, teacher, administrator or counselor shows the way. Many times however, the child gets little or no instruction on how to win in school.

Along with teaching academics, parents expect teachers to instruct students on how to survive in school. Conversely, teachers expect parents, before students come to school, already to have directed and instructed the child in the rules of the game called "school." However, many parents do not devote the time or don't know how to teach their children how to survive successfully in school. Perhaps the parents have had a poor school experience themselves or they are not interested. Either way, many times, students are not taught how to learn effectively and to be successful in school.

Despite strong research support for teaching responsibility and study skill strategies to students, it is apparently not done frequently in the context of K-12 education. In their review of research, Edward Shapiro and Christine Cole (1994) explain:

Although educational personnel and parents alike agree that learning self-management skills is a priority for children, these skills are seldom systematically taught to students, especially to those students with academic or behavior problems. The more typical emphasis has been on methods of classroom control and discipline using teacher-managed contingencies. (p.2)

Children enter the system and by the 5th grade, instead of moving up, students are looking for a way out. By graduation as many as thirty-three out of a hundred of beginning kindergarten students are gone (Education Week, 2003). Where did they go? They dropped out along the way and see themselves as failures.

They didn't know how to succeed in school and were not coached to win. This experience has left a bitter taste in their mouths. Unfortunately for us, many have vowed that they will never go back to that 'educational restaurant.' They have not been fed or nurtured. In addition, they are customers and parents of customers who will not recommend our nutritious educational establishment to others. Is it any wonder we are having concerns in American public education?

We cannot afford this waste of human potential in American education. While much of the discourse in boards of education and state governments across this country is about standards and raising scores on state mandated tests, we are missing the root of improving student achievement and creating life-long learners. We need to be about the task of developing life-long learners who, as a by-product of their labor, score well on the established standards for each grade level.

This Program is a time-tested attempt to systemize the "making of students." It is a survival program for students, teachers, and parents. It begins at the elementary level, right where it needs to start. It is research based and it is built upon basic truths about learning.

It promotes the other side of the coin of classroom management, and that is the responsibility of students to contribute to the good functioning of the classroom. The Program challenges students to be personally responsible for their learning by teaching them the survival tools necessary to win in school.

It highly values student choice, along with a veneration of teachers and learning. It acknowledges obedience growing from

★ INTRODUCTION (CONTINUED)

respect. It encourages and promotes effort from students. It believes in positive recognition based on achieved personal goals. It is uplifting and encouraging. It believes in possibilities and student potential. Finally, it is passionate about achievement and the reverence for teaching and learning.

Great schools are about the task of making higher-level thinkers and life-long learners—true **Super Students**. Super Students have certain qualities and behaviors that they use consciously and unconsciously. They have developed a repertoire of skills that they use on a daily basis. These skills continually build self-confidence and self-esteem. These skills can and must be taught by professional educators in our schools today. It is part of our obligation as professional educators.

Students are rewarded daily for these skills by teachers, staff, and parents/guardians. Consequently, they are successful in school and they are happy. They feel like they are in control. Nothing succeeds like success, and they have found the magic ingredient!

Super Students are not necessarily the top scoring students in the class. They are students who are respectful. They are always giving their best, trusting the teacher to lead along the way. They are students that are always pushing themselves further and further. They are winning in school! Why? They believe in themselves because someone has first believed in them and has taught them the skills to survive in school. Super Students are made not born.

Currently, we are not showing children how to survive in school. The statistics and research bear this out. In the results of the *Coleman Report* (Coleman, Campbell, Hobson, McPartland, Mood, Weinfield, & York, 1996), and *A Nation at Risk: The Imperative for Educational Reform* issued by the National Commission on Excellence in Education, were considered by some as proof that K-12 education had indeed dissolved to a state of irreversible disrepair. The effects of the report were profound, due in no small part, to the fact that it was perceived as the sanctioned opinion of the White House. David Berliner and Bruce Biddle note this in their book *The Manufactured Crisis: Myths, Frauds, and Attacks on America's Public Schools* (Berliner & Biddle, 1995).

The *Super Student Program* is a program designed to improve student achievement and behavior. For students, basic Super Student skills are introduced through three engaging and interactive stories. Each story is designed for a particular grade level. Activity sheets accompany each of the skills throughout the stories. Presented in a club format, the students are invited to join the "The Super Student Club" at the end of the story. The committed members are then presented the Super Student Focus Sheet, pledge, membership card and certificate. During the course of each marking period of the school year they are invited to renew their membership and commitment as teachers work with the concepts during their community circle time. The program for the students takes only fifteen to twenty minutes twice a week for five weeks. A celebration ceremony at the end of each marking period is highly recommended to recognize the achievements of these Super Students.

The program also contains a parent and teacher section. It invites parents to be partners with the school in raising a Super Student. Helpful hints for parents are included in the Program in a section entitled "A Survival Kit for the Parents." Parents are also invited to help their children memorize the Super Student Focus Skills and Pledge.

For the teacher, a section called "A Survival Kit for the Teacher" introduces eight steps to develop Super Students in the classroom. Helpful hints and techniques to be a master teacher and developer of Super Students are included.

INTRODUCTION (CONTINUED)

The program is built on some truths about learning. It highly values student choice, along with reverence for teachers and learning. It acknowledges obedience growing from respect. It encourages and promotes effort from students. It believes in positive recognition based on achieved personal goals. It is positive and encouraging. It believes in possibilities and student potential. Finally, it is passionate about learning and achievement.

Great schools are about the task of making thinkers, achievers and lifelong learners. These are true Super Students. Super Students have certain qualities and skills that they use consciously and unconsciously in school. They have developed a repertoire of skills that they use on a daily basis with success. These skills continually build self-confidence and self-esteem in a school setting.

Students are rewarded daily for these skills consciously and unconsciously by teachers, staff, and parents/guardians. Consequently, they are successful in school and they are happy. They feel like they are in control. As the saying goes, nothing promotes success like success, and they have found the magic key!

The qualities and traits necessary to be successful in school can and must be taught in a systematic way. All educators need to be "stirring the same stew" as they prepare learners. We owe it to our children to equip them to be successful in one of the most important experiences of their lives. They cannot be students that simply 'muddle through,' or worse, fail and quit. They must be *Super Students* who know why they are in school, love to come, learn, and respect their teachers. As a byproduct, they will score well on any test appropriate for their grade level.

This Program will focus on the process and skills necessary for learning in an institutional setting so that students can achieve their full potential. They will then return to that 'educational gourmet restaurant' over and over again to taste the best that life has to offer.

★ RATIONALE

Imagine working in a rural school in South Carolina where 88% of your students are on free or reduced-price lunch and 90% of the students are from homes where the biological fathers or mothers are not present. The *Super Student Program and Club* were tested and used extensively at Green Sea Floyds Elementary School (GSFE) in Horry County, SC from 1999 to 2004.

Green Sea Floyds Elementary is a rural elementary school with a population of 700 students in grades Child Development to 6th grade. The teachers at GSFE are hard working and dedicated to helping children succeed. GSFE won the Palmetto Gold Award for major improvement in statewide testing in 2002. Then, in 2003, we received the Palmetto Silver Award. During these past two years, our discipline problems were cut by more than 1/3. More students than ever have won Renaissance/Celebration Awards. These recognition awards are based on achievement and behavior. They are given every nine weeks at report card time. Now, 70% of our population wins Renaissance/Celebration Awards. Whereas four years ago, only 30% of the population received the award. The Palmetto Gold and Silver Awards given by the state place GSFE as one of the finest rural schools in SC.

I developed the *Super Student Program and Club* over the course of thirty-five years in public education and refined them during the last eight years. They were an outgrowth of earlier concepts developed in an American Guidance Service published program, *Peer Pals* (Bowman & Chanaca, 1994). These concepts have been further developed in the *Super Student Program*. They were further refined as I studied the work of Marzano, Pickering, and Pollock (2001) in their work, *Classroom Instruction that Works*. (Research Based Strategies for Increasing Student Achievement).

In Marzano, Pickering, and Pollock's (2001) work, the researchers at Midcontinent Research for Education and Learning (McREL) analyzed selected research studies on instructional strategies that could be used by teachers in K-12 classrooms. In effect, they summarized all the research for the last thirty years concerning what makes a school effective in producing students with high achievement.

One of the primary goals of the McREL study was to identify those instructional strategies that have the highest probability of enhancing student achievement for all students in all subject areas at all grade levels. Marzano identified nine categories of strategies that have the strongest effect on producing high student achievement. Interestingly enough, the third most important category identified is reinforcing student effort and providing recognition for attaining educational goals. He found these two elements to be imperative for a quality school to exist. Twenty-one studies were analyzed with remarkable conclusions for educators. First, the research on effort produced two major generalizations (Marzano 2001).

1. **Not all students realized the importance of believing in effort.**
Although obvious to adults, particularly successful ones, effort pays off in terms of enhanced achievement. Not all students are aware of this. In fact, studies have demonstrated that some students are not aware that effort they put into a task has a direct effect on their success relative to the task (see Seligman, 1990,1994; Urdan, Midgley, &Anderman, 1998). The implication here is that teachers should explain and exemplify the "effort belief" to students. The *Super Student Program* does this repeatedly throughout the program, lessons, stories, and activities.

2. **Students can learn to change their beliefs.**
Probably, one of the most promising aspects of the research on effort is that students can learn to operate from the belief that effort pays off, even if they do not initially have this belief. This is the major educational finding that supports the *Super Student Program's* rationale. An interesting set of studies has shown that simply demonstrating that added

⭐ RATIONALE *(CONTINUED)*

effort will pay off in terms of enhanced achievement (see Craske, 1985; Wilson & Linville, 1982). (Van Overwalle & Demetsenaere, 1990) found that students who were taught about the relationship between effort and achievement increased their achievement more than students who were taught techniques for time management and comprehension of new materials.

The direct implications of these two major discoveries undergird the effectiveness of the *Super Student Program*. The program emphasizes sustained student effort and perseverance through its stories as it presents personal study skills for students to master. I am pleased that the *Super Student Program* is strongly based on the principles supported by the McREL study. This is the most significant study in education during the last thirty years.

When the *Super Student Program* is coupled with public recognition, every marking period throughout the year, student achievement is even more positively effected. Many years of research have demonstrated that behavior that is rewarded tends to continue, whereas behavior that is ignored tends to diminish (Hoppin and Splete, 1996).

Major generalizations were extracted from "providing recognition" as a category of instructional strategies from Marzano's (2001) research for increasing student achievement. While all the generalizations apply to the effectiveness of the *Super Student Program*, the second concept is of particular interest. It states that rewards are most effective when they are contingent on the attainment of some standard of performance. Studies by Wiersma (1992) and by Cameron and Pierce (1994) both provide additional support for the generalization that rewards work fairly well when they are based on the attainment of some performance standard or goal.

Basically, the research findings confirm that teachers, on a regular and consistent basis, need to emphasize student effort and reinforce the link between effort and success if educators want an effective school. Then, they must provide continuous recognition of attained academic goals.

The *Super Student Program* deals primarily with this finding and provides for both aspects of this category. Reinforcing effort with the *Super Student Program* can help teach one of the most valuable lessons students can learn: **The harder you try at school tasks, the more success you will achieve.** In addition, providing recognition for the attainment of specific goals or skills not only enhances achievement, but it stimulates motivation (Marzano 2001).

The Super Student concepts work! They will turn a school around or maintain a school's winning course if the most important people-the teachers and staff-stay focused on the program and persevere throughout the school year. These concepts become a survival kit for students, teachers, and parents as they are employed and promoted.

When thinking of survival, thoughts go to the essentials that allow people to succeed on a daily basis. This is what the *Super Student Program* does. It focuses on the most essential elements that make good students. If these skills are used on a habitual basis, they will provide a framework on which achievement in a classroom or a school can build to go far beyond survival. It will bring your class or school to mastery and excellence.

My thirty-five years of experience as a teacher and counselor have been infused into the program. My belief in the importance of the roles the children, teachers, and parents each have to play is fully expressed in this survival kit. I have a love for children and a belief in their vast potential, which can be fully harnessed by the concepts and skills presented in this Program. This Program is one of the first of its kind to challenge students to be responsible personally for their learning. In addition, it provides the tools to develop personal power for each student to control their education. It produces students who can take full advantage of this great American educational experience that we call school.

© Youthlight, Inc.

ELEMENTS OF THE PROGRAM

★ Objective

The *Super Student Program* was developed to help students:

- **Take responsibility for their learning.**
- **Learn a systematic method for improving their schoolwork.**
- **Improve effort toward academic tasks.**
- **Absorb basic study skills and concepts that improve the effectiveness and efficiency of their learning.**
- **Enhance self-esteem in the learning experience.**
- **Develop into life-long learners with positive, healthy attitudes.**

★ The four parts to the *Super Student Program*

1. **The Stories and Lessons**
2. **The Super Student Club and Awards Celebration**
3. **The Survival Kit for the Teacher**
4. **The Survival Kit for the Parent**

Stories and Lessons

The stories in this Program are presented in mini-lessons for your class. These ten lessons will prepare your students to form the *Super Student Club*. The stories/lessons contain all the work you would normally do during a shared reading time or language arts period with your students in a community circle atmosphere. Teachers consider it part of their reading program. So, you are doing academics while you are working with the *Super Student Program*!

Each grade level section has a short introduction and then presents the particular Super Student story to the students. The stories are different for each level, but they each deal with the same Super Student Focus Skills and Super Student concepts. They are enjoyable, illustrated and interactive.

Appropriate questions at the end of each lesson are available for the teacher to use to further build the concepts presented. Also, additional activities are included to develop your students into great students.

We encourage two sessions per week. These sessions will take only 15-20 minutes during your community circle for approximately five weeks. Preferably, you will run your community circle on Monday and Wednesday mornings. This will give you the alternate days to use the follow up Skills Sheets and activities as if you were conducting a language arts activity. The lessons will allow you to develop the Super Student skills and concepts which your children will need as they stay focused on the essentials of winning in school.

Please note where to start in the following three sections and the grade levels.

SUPER STUDENT STORIES

- Story: The Key Maker (Grades K-1)
- Story: Talon and The Magic Eggs (Grades 2-3)
- Story: The Old Man (Grades 4-5)

ELEMENTS OF THE PROGRAM (CONT.)

Skills and Pledge

★ **SUPER STUDENT FOCUS SKILLS FOR GRADES K–1**

1. I will listen, obey, and trust my teacher.
2. I will raise my hand to speak.
3. I will give my best.
4. I will finish all my work.
5. I will work out problems with others.
6. I will have a positive, healthy attitude.

(See Black line masters for student copy)

★ **SUPER STUDENT FOCUS SKILLS FOR GRADES 2-6**

1. I will listen, obey, and trust my teacher.
2. I will raise my hand to speak.
3. I will think along with the speaker.
4. I will be prepared for my work.
5. I will give my best.
6. I will finish all my work.
7. I will work out problems with others.
8. I will have a positive, healthy attitude.

(See Black line Masters for student copy)

★ **THE SUPER STUDENT PLEDGE GRADES 2-5**

My attitude is the only thing I can control in life. I can choose to be happy or sad, helpful or hurtful. I can choose to be a winner in school. My attitude is reflected in these SUPER STUDENT FOCUS Skills. I will read these Focus Skills everyday. I will practice these skills to show I am a winner. People will see me doing these things, and good things will happen to me! I will be happy in school because of what I do and say. People are influenced by what I say and do. As I focus on these skills, I will feel happy inside. Being GOOD is good for me! I really want to be a winner in school.

(See Black line Master for student copy)

The Super Student Club and Awards Celebration

You will be inviting your class to join the *Super Student Club* at the end of the lessons. In most academic clubs, students are usually invited to join first and then learn what the club is about. The *Super Student Program* presents the challenge to students to be personally responsible for their learning by giving them the survival tools necessary to win in school. Then, it invites them to join the Club.

The students will sign a commitment and will practice the Super Student Focus Skills on a daily basis. Forms are available in the Program to monitor their growth.

Each classroom will have its own *Super Student Club* directed by the classroom teacher. Grade levels can combine for various occasions and the whole school *Super Student Club* will, of course, celebrate every marking period if a school chooses to go school wide with the *Super Student Program*. Again, I prefer that the whole school adopt the Program so the school will be unified in the building of students.

It is preferable for all students to memorize the Super Student Focus Skills and My Pledge (please note that the k-1 pledge is shorter than the other grades). Parents are asked in the letter to the parents to help with this at home (see the Black line masters for your particular level). Getting parent support for the Program is important. The Super Student

★ ELEMENTS OF THE PROGRAM (CONT.)

The Super Student Club and Awards Celebration
(cont.)

Program has a parent section called "A Survival Kit for the Parent."

Membership cards can be handed out and certificates (membership cards and certificates are included as Black line masters in the Program) and awards can be given at the end of each marking period. Students may use the Super Student Focus Skills and My Pledge sheets during the course of the grading period. They may be posted on their desks or work area. These sheets can be used as a guide or reference as the weeks go on, so students can be reminded how to be a Super Student on a daily basis.

The use of **The Super Student Focus Skills Checklist** (a Black line master) is highly recommended to get ready for the Awards Celebration. Have your students use this checklist at least twice a week to keep tabs on their attitude and behavior before the marking period is over. This checklist is very useful for arrangements that you have with parents on daily reports that need to go home concerning their student's behavior. This checklist is an excellent form to monitor your *Super Student Club* members before the Awards Celebration.

The Awards Celebration

It is strongly recommended that some sort of recognition program be used at the end of every marking period to reward and celebrate the Super Students in your school, even if it is only individual classrooms that are celebrating. School wide celebrations make the Program even stronger. After all, we are in the business of producing good students and life-long learners. We should celebrate our product!

The Celebration Program awards students for achievement as well as good behavior each grading period during the year. The award levels include gold cards for students with all A's and no discipline referrals, silver cards for students who made all A's and B's and have no discipline referrals. Finally, bronze cards (probably the most important card) for students whose teachers believe they are putting forth good effort and have a Super Student attitude, regardless of their grades. We allowed one discipline write-up per marking period for the bronze card but you can structure the criteria, as you would like.

The rewards of the Celebration Program can be plentiful, especially when your school gets businesses to support your program. They can include t-shirts, medals, cards, certificates, and free admissions to select sporting and community events. Local businesses are often eager to be involved in positive school/community projects like *The Super Student Program*.

Because of its focus on learning enhancement and motivation that will turn into high achievement results, businesses will offer funding and incentive items for the program. Make sure, however, that the businesses receive something in return. Free advertisement and your endorsement in the media are often attractive to businesses.

The awards ceremony at the end of each grading period is a major event to which parents and community members can and should be invited. If used school wide, usually an afternoon is blocked out with a special event, a special speaker, or music program. The Super Student Club provides a day-to-day build up and preparation for each of the grading periods and allows the Celebration Program to be a time to which students look forward.

We have found that the use of the *Super Student Program and Club* when linked with a strong Celebration Program can increase the achievement levels and decrease the discipline referrals significantly.

In addition to the Celebration Program every nine weeks, our pilot school developed a Hard Work Café. We had a beautiful courtyard that was not being used. We simply added beautiful tables and umbrellas, a fountain, benches, some landscaping and

ELEMENTS OF THE PROGRAM (CONT.)

started serving nutritious snacks during the day. What a privilege for a Super Student to come once a week to enjoy the Café for fifteen to twenty minutes and have a healthy snack. All the money we receive from the Hard Work Café is recycled back into the Super Student Program and Celebrations to buy medals, certificates, trophies and special guest performances.

Your celebrations at report card time will honor your Super Student Club members and draw in the community as you recognize your winners. By making a big deal out of your club members, others students will want to join the Super Student Club.

This preparation at the elementary level is vital in that students are reminded in a systematic way what a Super Student and Celebration winner focuses on each and every day. This will lead them to receiving future awards. The skills they are learning are reinforced so that the students at each level are developing the skills they need to be happy and successful in school.

The Survival Kit for the Teacher

The Program also contains a teacher and parent section.
For the teacher, a section called "A Survival Kit for the Teacher" introduces eight steps to develop Super Students in the classroom. Helpful hints and techniques to be a master teacher and developer of Super Students are included.

The Survival Kit for the Parent

For the parent, it invites parents to be partners with the school in raising a Super Student. Helpful hints for parents are included in the Program in a section entitled "A Survival Kit for the Parents." Parents are also invited to help their children memorize the Super Student Focus Skills and My Pledge.

Summary

This Program is for all students. It is a program that challenges the student to have a great responsibility for his/her learning and the proper functioning of the class. *The Super Student Program* will make poor learners into good learners and good learners into great ones! It revolutionizes the thinking of all students because it holds them personally responsible for their learning. It is the other side of the coin in excellent classroom management.

It will also give teachers, staff, and parents a place to start when they say to a student, "You need to be a better student." The student wonders, "Why should I? Where do I start? What do I have to do to be a good student? What are the skills I need to be successful?"

Think of your classroom as a gourmet kitchen ready to make beautiful and delicious meals. Your environment must be inviting, you must have the correct tools and materials, and you, as chief chef must prepare the various components in a certain order and in a certain way to achieve the greatest dining experience!

You will have to assemble the ingredients before you begin to concoct the epicurean repast. Elements will have to be cut, sliced, diced and julienned. Only then, will you be able to create your masterpiece.

There is a chemistry involved in cooking. After excellent preparation, when all the elements are blended in the correct proportions at the right time, magic occurs! It is the same in the classroom between teacher and student. It is the magic of learning!

★ QUESTIONS AND ANSWERS
For the Professional Educator

Before you begin, here are some important questions you will want answered:

1. What should I do if all students do not join the Club after all the mini-lessons are given?

One of the most important concepts of this program is the matter of student choice. This Program highly promotes the other side of classroom management, and that is the responsibility of students to contribute to the proper functioning of the classroom. It is long over-due in American education. This concept will be drilled over and over in the mini-lessons. It is the author's belief that children's choices must be honored and that they must be held responsible for their choices. Choices such as whether or not to do school work, to listen or not to listen, to hit someone or not to hit, have consequences. Until children feel the weight of natural and logical consequences, they do not "own" their behavior. This does not mean that we would put children in dangerous situations to work out these solutions, but reasonable, real life situations in school present a great learning environment for students to develop decision making skills.

Teachers need to respect a student's choice even if it does not seem positive. Letting students know that they have choices gives those students power over their lives and does not hold you responsible for the choices that they make. It holds the students responsible.

It is my experience that most students will join something that is exciting, positive, and for their benefit. If a student persists in not being involved, ask why privately. Explore it together. Encourage other students to go to the student to secure his/her commitment to be in the Club. This positive peer pressure can be powerful and useful in securing the membership of all students in the program. Even so, if a student does not want to be a Super Student after all this, honor their choice and continue to leave the door open for him/her to join later.

2. How do I keep the flow of the Program going for five weeks?

All master teachers have used a community circle in the morning or the afternoon to start or sum up the day. Going over the agenda for the day, focusing on getting along with classmates, and sharing important information about upcoming events is all part of excellent teaching. We advise speaking about the Super Student Club and the Super Student Skills, along with the stories for each skill, daily. After all, we are trying to develop Super Students. It is what schools are about! This daily reminder is what students need. Since most of the Super Student concepts hit on these areas, use this opportunity to bring out the times you have caught your students being good in class. Use their Super Student Focus Skill Sheets to point out these good skills. I believe that teachers need to stress 'catching students being good' on a regular, ongoing basis. The stories are presented in a reading/language arts format and take only 15-20 minutes a lesson, so you are doing academics while you are presenting the Program. The stories are very engaging and easily hold the students' attention.

Also, on Friday afternoons, provide a time for the Super Student Club to meet. It will be a time to review the week with the Super Student Focus Skill Sheet, activity sheets, and plan service-learning projects for the school and community.

At our pilot school, we developed a Hard Work Café. Any classroom teacher could use our open courtyard with tables and umbrellas once a week if their students had worked like Super Students. We would serve nutritious drinks and snacks. The students could bring books to read and enjoy reading during their time off. We will have more on this later. This celebrates good students. You will need to celebrate your Super Students as they continue to grow.

QUESTIONS AND ANSWERS (CONT.)
For the Professional Educator

3. What effect does it have when I notice students being "super"?

Many teachers will post rules and regulations at the beginning of the school year with good intentions and then use a point or take away system when these rules are broken. The system works well for the teachers because it is easier to look for bad behavior than to catch kids being good. It is convenient.

The problem occurs when three or four students are having problems and they catch on to the fact that they can invite the teacher to notice them in a negative way. The *Super Student Program* emphasizes that "catching students being good" is far more effective.

When students are rewarded for earning something, they own the good behavior and it builds their self-esteem and confidence. Also, giving something to someone after he/she has performed well is psychologically more positive than taking something away.

The research by Marzano (2001) proves it is far more effective to plan with the students at the beginning of the year the rules that will make their classroom effective and safe. Then spend your time 'catching your students being good'.

At the beginning of the year, have your students help you form the rules for the class during community circle. These rules will be very similar, if not identical, to the rules that you would have posted the first day of class. They are now 'their rules.' They have formed them and voted on them. They now have ownership of the rules as a class family. If you look closely, the rules that the students have chosen will be very similar to the Super Student Focus Skills in the Program.

4. Should parents be involved?

Absolutely! You can go beyond what is recommended, but this program will provide for it. The *Super Student Program* and its companion program, *Peer Pals* have been welcomed in the schools that have used it. It can easily become part of a school's showcase of unique learning and achievement enhancement efforts.

When the *Super Student Program* is combined with a recognition program every report card period, the results are impressive. Invite parents to the celebration of your Super Students at the end of each marking period during your recognition program. Giving medals, certificates, using cheerleaders, and taking pictures are impressive ways to involve your parents in the Super Student Program. The program can help promote an understanding in the community that a school is continuing to search for and use more effective ways to help children become better learners. It values their involvement in the partnership of educating their children.

To implement any new program, it is recommended that leaders first work to build support among administrators, teachers, students, parents, local business members, and the local media.

5. How can teachers and counselors build support for the program?

While single classrooms would, of course, benefit from using the *Super Student Program* and the concepts that it promotes, total school or grade level adoption is the preferred way to achieve maximum school-wide change. In addition, the culmination of three to four years of use will start to produce long-term Super Students and attitudes that will effect the whole school and community.

Any winning coach will tell you that a comprehensive program that produces winning

QUESTIONS AND ANSWERS (CONT.)
for the Professional Educator

attitudes will, after a while, start to change a community's attitude about itself. This is exactly what the *Super Student Program* does.

When a teacher begins to think like a winner and begins to have winning experiences, that teacher will act like a winner. Your students will follow your lead. You will need support to launch the *Super Student Program* either in your classroom or school-wide. Let's look at administrative, teacher, student, parent, and local community/business support.

Administrative Support. Support from the school administration for this program is critical for its overall success. The *Super Student Program* needs to be presented to administrators as part of your school's overall academic program.

It fits well into the counseling/guidance program, but the *Super Student Program* is most influential when the classroom teacher delivers it during the community circle or discussion time. The classroom is where the power of any program lies and the teacher is the driving force in the classroom. Counselors can assist in the school wide effort to drive the Program and use the Program in small groups and individual counseling sessions.

Administrators, this program works well to enhance student learning and achievement by teaching Super Student study skills and by improving attitudes toward learning. As a result, achievement and behavior will improve. You need to be aware that by adopting this program, you will provide the professional staff with a collective definition of "winning in school." The *Super Student* concepts and skills that focus on positive attitudes toward learning in school and lifelong learning will be a part of everyone's vocabulary.

Besides improving student achievement, the *Super Student Program* will diminish your discipline problems. As students take school more seriously and many start to grow into happy, successful students the Program will start to seriously effect your discipline numbers. Students will try to get into the Super Student Club so they will be celebrated every report card time. You will have a winning school especially if you build up the celebrations into community and child center recognition programs that are remembered as exciting and enjoyable events.

Administrators today need a program that unifies the school and celebrates winning. The *Super Student Program* can define winning in school for an entire school or district. The by-products are higher test scores and happier students and teachers!

Teacher Support. Initiating the program with the teachers who have the greatest receptiveness and interest would be best. First, explain to them the program's objectives and format. Emphasize that this is a valuable use of students' time. The stories in the program that deliver the concepts are engaging and fit into any reading program.

Students who are participating are "learning about learning." They are acquiring basic skills and tools that will help them to develop a positive attitude about school and achievement.

Show the teachers the Leader's Guide and the elements of the Program. Skim over any of the three stories that deliver the Program. Note how interesting and interactive the stories are. In addition, the stories fit into any language arts program so your teachers are doing academics while they are building Super Students. Help the teachers discover how beneficial the Program is for students and how user-friendly the Program is for them.

When teachers are aware of the *Super Student Program's* potential and short time investment, they will embrace using the Super Student Club and Awards Celebration all year long. The *Super Student Program* is a survival kit for students, teachers, and parents. In today's classroom, most teachers will welcome proven ways to make winners in

QUESTIONS AND ANSWERS (CONT.)
For the Professional Educator

their classrooms. Finally, note that the Program has a teacher and parent survival kit included.

Parent Support. Sending the prepared parent letters informing them about the *Super Student Program* is vital to the success of the program (See Black line masters). The letters will give some basic information about the Program and its objectives. It will also invite them to a meeting so you can share an overview about how they can reinforce the eight focus skills and the pledge that you are teaching their children.

In addition, your principal, counselor, curriculum coordinator or home/school coordinator can use the last section of our program to continue to work with "The Survival Kit for Parents." This section of the Program is invaluable as you secure your parents as partners in the *Super Student Program*.

Finally, after the end of the ten lessons, a letter is sent home to the parents to secure them as partners. They will help with the memorization of the Super Student Focus Skills and Pledge.

You may reproduce the letter as it is or adapt it to your needs. Enlisting parents' help will be easier if you emphasize that the *Super Student Program* works to enhance student learning and achievement by teaching skills that improve attitude toward learning, self-esteem and motivation. When these items improve, high achievement follows.

Local Community and Business Support. Local businesses are often eager to be involved in positive school/community projects like *The Super Student Program*. Because of its focus on learning enhancement and motivation that will turn into high achievement results, businesses will offer funding and incentive items for the program. Make sure, however, that the businesses receive something in return. Free advertisement and your endorsement in the media are often attractive to businesses.

6. What is a Super Student?

I believe that any student can become a Super Student. Great students are made not born. It is all about a super attitude! Part of the job we have as professional educators is to develop and help construct a positive healthy attitude that causes students to soar and become all that they can be. A Super Student has a positive attitude about the possibilities of school and learning. He/she is respectful. This student is always giving his/her best, trusting the teacher to lead the way. He/she is always pushing himself/herself further. Achievement is a natural byproduct of this super attitude.

These students are winning in school and have learned the skills that make good things happen to them. They believe in themselves. In short, they have learned how to be successful and happy in school. They have learned how to focus on forming certain habits that continue to cause them to win in school. Most times, good grades and high achievement test scores are the result of this kind of attitude. Most of all, the warm feeling of having done one's best is evident in all students. They are happy to come to school to be nurtured, and they will use the skills they learn throughout their lives.

7. What are the eight Super Student Focus Skills?

1. I will listen, obey, and trust my teacher.
2. I will raise my hand to speak.
3. I will think along with the speaker.
4. I will be prepared with my homework.
5. I will give my best.
6. I will finish all my work.
7. I will work out problems with others.
8. I will have a positive, healthy attitude.

QUESTIONS AND ANSWERS (CONT.)
For the Professional Educator

8. What are the Program's objectives?

The *Super Student Program* was developed to help students:

- Take responsibility for their learning.
- Learn a systematic model for improving their schoolwork.
- Improve effort toward academic tasks.
- Absorb basic study skills and concepts that improve the effectiveness and efficiency of their learning.
- Enhance self-esteem in the learning experience.
- Develop into life-long learners with positive, healthy attitudes.

9. What is the purpose of the Super Student Skill Sheets and activities?

After the students are introduced to the eight skills, they need time to practice and use the skills to become comfortable and proficient with them. They do this with the Super Student Skill Sheets and the activities that are provided. In kindergarten and 1st grade, they will have symbols that will remind them of the skills. In grades two through five, the skill sheets and activities are more interactive. In addition, at the end of the week, the teacher can encourage and promote the use of the skills on a regular basis so that these skills can become routine. The color levels in the stories give the students a reference point to track their growth as a Super Student. Then, when they reach the Black level, they will be ready to share what they have learned with others and join the Super Student Club.

All the Super Student Skill Sheets and the activities are reproducible as Black line masters so they can be used over and over.

10. How does the *Super Student Program* apply to at-risk students?

While the *Super Student Program* is a program for <u>all</u> students, it was my purpose for this Program to have special value for at-risk students. It can be a survival kit for them as well! It teaches that all students can choose to win at the 'game called school.' It gives them the tools to accomplish this task in a simple and direct manner which they can learn, practice, and demonstrate. They can learn to make themselves happy in school in spite of their circumstance in life. Their attitudes will make the difference! This Program has been used in special education programs that employ daily token systems with wonderful success. Also, behavioral intervention plans (BIP) have been developed using the Focus Skills and My Pledge with tremendous success.

11. What benefits do students receive?

When children first enter school, they learn about learning in an institution with groups of students. An effective enhancement program for children must have two fundamental components. It must begin by ensuring that students believe they are capable learners. Then, it needs to provide strategies they can use to help them become better learners and achievers in school.

The *Super Student Program* has these two components. It helps children to build more positive beliefs about their ability to learn. It also provides strategies that can enable children to increase their number of successes in their schoolwork. Finally, the *Super Student Program* honors student choice.

The Program teaches that learning is important and that all students can choose to be winners in school. It emphasizes that past failure need not be discouraging and that learning requires an ability to put effort into

© Youthlight, Inc.

QUESTIONS AND ANSWERS (CONT.)
for the Professional Educator

all tasks, even tasks that aren't fun. It proves that effort pays off. Also, it insists that they must take responsibility for the choices they make regarding their learning.

Everyday, students make many such choices. They choose how much time and effort to put into working on different classroom tasks, how much to allow the teacher to direct their learning experiences, and how they direct their own learning experiences outside the classroom. The teacher can lead and needs to offer something to the student to change negative behavior.

The *Super Student Program* now permits the teacher to offer a student a way out of negative behaviors while holding that student personally responsible for the choices he/she makes.

12. How much time does the program require?

This Program will require training for your students. We are suggesting 15 to 20 minutes a session during community circle twice a week for five weeks. The stories at the various levels carry the skills and the message of the Program so you are still teaching academics. The lessons are the same as guided reading lessons with questions and skill sheets. That works out to approximately ten sessions, depending on the level or grade. In that way, the concepts can be shared, practiced and learned. This is a small investment of time for great returns. The skill sheets for grades two through five should be used on alternate days to firm up the skill being introduced. For continued success, you will need to revisit the Super Student Focus Skills and My Pledge throughout the year. Also, every marking period should be a celebration period for each Super Student. This should be done in front of the class, grade or school with the parents/guardians invited for the celebration.

13. How can the Super Student Program fuse with Jostens' Renaissance Program as a winning combination to increase learning for an entire school?

You can form your own Awards Celebration as I have already mentioned. We did ours with free assistance from Jostens'. The Celebration Program in combination with the Super Student Program/Club is an awesome pairing. The free Jostens' Renaissance Program has been called, 'one of the most positive developments on the American educational landscape in the last ten years'. As the name indicates, the drive behind the Renaissance idea is the rebirth of the educational mission in America. It is FREE for school districts to use.

© Youthlight, Inc.

QUESTIONS AND ANSWERS *(CONT.)*
For the Professional Educator

Renaissance uses reward and recognition to generate energy, motivation, and commitment. It enjoys support from all sectors of the community: students, faculties, parents, local governments, and businesses. It is 'academics with an attitude!'

The Renaissance Program awards students for achievement as well as good behavior each grading period during the year. The award levels include gold cards for students with all A's and no discipline referrals, silver cards for students who made all A's and B's and have no discipline referrals and bronze cards (probably the most important card) for students whose teachers believe they are putting forth good effort and have a Super Student attitude regardless of their grades.

The rewards of the Renaissance Program can be plentiful, especially when your school gets businesses to support your program. They can include t-shirts, medals, cards, certificates, and free admissions to select sporting and community events. The awards ceremony at the end of each grading period is a major event to which parents and community members can be invited. Usually, an afternoon is blocked out with a special event, such as a special speaker or music program. *The Super Student Club* provides a day-to-day build up and preparation for each of the grading periods.

This preparation at the elementary level is vital in that students are reminded in a systematic way what a Super Student and Renaissance winner focuses on each and every day. This will lead them to receiving Renaissance awards. The skills they are learning are reinforced so that the students at each level are developing the skills they need to be happy and successful in school.

The *Super Student Club* and its concepts become a survival kit for students, teachers, and parents. For more information on starting your free Renaissance Program to coordinate with the *Super Student Program* contact Jostens at 1-800-235-4774 ext. 3245.

It is strongly recommended that some sort of recognition program be used at the end of every marking period to reward and celebrate the best students in your school. You can use your current marking period celebration and just build into it.

In addition to the Awards Celebration, our pilot school developed a Hard Work Café. We had a beautiful courtyard that was not being used. We simply added tables and umbrellas, a fountain, benches, some landscaping and started serving nutritious snacks during the day. What a privilege for a Super Student to come once a week to enjoy the Café for fifteen to twenty minutes and have a healthy snack. All the money we receive from the Hard Work Café is recycled back into the Super Student Program Celebrations to buy medals, certificates, trophies and special guest performances.

ADAPTING THE PROGRAM
For Small Groups & Individual Help

One of the advantages of the Super Student Program is its flexibility. While it can be used effectively with whole classrooms to strengthen a total school program of achievement and management, it can also be used with small groups or in individual situations. Any of the appropriate stories or activities can be used in any particular school situation. Going over the story parts for a specific group or individual concern has been very successful in our pilot programs.

Full time special education classes and resource room situations have used the Super Student Program very effectively. In fact, because special education situations are generally intensive learning situations, the Super Student Program is even more effective. In these intense situations, the teacher and students use it with more vigor. When students in these intensive situations are rewarded on a daily basis, their behavior and personal ownership of classroom management improves more quickly. We have seen special education classes turn around completely when the Super Student Focus Skills are reinforced on a daily basis and the students are recognized for their achievements.

The Super Student Program has been use in Behavioral Intervention Programs (BIP) for special education students and in behavioral contracts for regular education students. Because the Super Student Focus Skills are so specific, they are very effective in monitoring a student's progress on an hourly or daily basis. Students can receive points or tokens if they are doing the skills for whatever interval that would be appropriate for the particular student. The students then redeem their tokens or points for prizes in our Super Student Store.

All of the worksheets in the Black line section of the program are effective when dealing with special education students.

The Program is highly effective in school and mental health counseling situations. Because the Program was developed as an outgrowth of counseling needs that I was constantly dealing with in my role as counselor in elementary schools, I developed the concepts and used the earlier versions from a global elementary experience. In short, I was effective in dealing with problem students who were not Super Students by sharing the Super Student Focus Skills and the activities that are in the Program. This Program is effective because it personally challenges every student with his or her part in the learning experience.

The Program challenges each student with the fact that they are in charge of their learning. It holds them accountable for their part of classroom management.

The Super Student Program has a teacher survival section with eight magic ideas to develop Super Student in their class.

Finally, the Super Student Program has a parenting component that allows parents to become partners with the school as both develop the Super Student that they want. Prepared materials for PTA meetings make the Super Student Program flexible and adaptable for schools as they embrace the power of parental influence in developing good students.

The SUPER STUDENT Program
LEADER'S GUIDE FOR GRADES K-1

Rationale

The primary grades, kindergarten and beginning first grade are very special and offer an opportune time to develop young Super Students. These students are filled with energy and excitement for learning and interacting. They are highly motivated and influenced greatly by your energy and excitement. They are highly impressionable. The early years present a great challenge for educators to lay a foundation of habits, beliefs and attitudes that will follow the young learner throughout his/her life.

Getting these young students to learn in a group takes patience and persistence. Many of the students with whom I have come in contact have never been told 'no' at home, not to mention, how to sit, behave, listen or participate in a group-learning environment. When we put them in these situations, of course, they do not know how to act. I believe that all students, especially very young ones, need to start the process of group learning and positive behaviors in a group at the beginning of their school experience.

If these group skills are not taught, even for brief moments, students in these lower grades learn to yell out, interrupt the teacher and other students, and talk to monopolize the discussion in selfish ways. Their behavior becomes habitual. If they are instructed in positive, healthy group learning behavior, they will enjoy exploring and sharing together with other students and their teachers. This author is in no way trying to stifle or retard young students' expression and excitement for learning. Students need the spontaneity and wonderment that comes from exploratory learning. However, group learning requires a certain set of rules or skills to be effective. While all great learning activities are not always group activities, good educators will, at times, pull large or small groups together to introduce or build on a concept.

Group sessions are the teachable moments for Super Student behavior. Nurture these skills and they grow. Celebrate them and they remain. These skills will become the survival tool kit for these students as they progress through the lower grades. They will become habitual for most students.

While computer programs will be helpful and individual projects and exploration will be profitable, group learning and sharing will be the special time when self-esteem grows and learning from and with others begins.

'All knowing' is not my definition of a Super Student. To be able to take instruction and direction, to be able to solve problems, to be mannerly and respectful, to give one's best is what is needed. To be able to work out problems with others, ask appropriate questions, to be persistent and, most importantly, to posses a positive, healthy attitude–these are the skills that will produce Super Students who are winners in school and in everyday life.

I believe that true education brings young students from irresponsible to responsible, from immature to mature, from selfish to unselfish, and from unknowing to knowledgeable. It is in the group setting (school) that students learn about community, appreciation for others, and problem solving that benefits others.

© Youthlight, Inc.

★ K-1 LEADER'S GUIDE (CONT.)

They will need academic and social skills to be successful. Students need to know how to survive in a group and how to win in a school setting. These are skills that all winners use in school to make school the most profitable setting possible.

Please note that at the primary level (K-1) the *Super Student Program* will have only six skills to master. The reinforcement is done by key symbols that denote each skill. Two additional skills: "I will think along with the speaker" and "I will be prepared for my work" are taught in grades two and above. This gives a total of eight skills from grades two to six to master in the *Super Student Program*. These grades (2-5) have follow-up activity skill sheets that are vital for reinforcement of each of the eight skills.

The activity skill sheets are used the day after the skill is presented in the story. This gives a great follow up opportunity to drive home the skill and the commitment. All of this is done during your community circle or shared reading time. The stories are interesting and contain all the work you would normally do during a shared reading time with your students. Consider it part of your reading program. So, you are doing academics while you are working with the Program!

Getting Started

Now you are ready to start the story, lessons, and activities that will lead your students to join the *Super Student Club*. The preparation for the Program for the students takes only fifteen to twenty minutes twice a week for five weeks. All of this is done during your community circle or shared reading time. Have fun and enjoy the making of Super Students!

Story: The KEY MAKER

Use this for grades **Kindergarten and 1st grade**. This story will be read to students in a group situation. It would be best to have the students sit on a carpet or floor in front of you. A community circle with a family atmosphere is recommended. Of course, discuss any of the illustrations as they apply to the story.

Introduction

THE LEADER SAYS:

"Today class, we are going to start an adventure. I am starting a Super Student Club and would like everyone to join! Our club will do exciting projects and each one of its members will learn how to win and be happy in school. I will teach anyone who wants to be a Super Student the skills necessary to win in school.

My problem is that I can't make you join. It is a choice you will have to make by yourself. I would like everyone to be in the club, but I cannot make you be in it. I would like to tell you about the club and what a Super Student is. Then, after you have heard all about the Program, I will invite you to sign up to be a member. Would you like to hear more about our club and what you have to do to be a member? Good! Let's get started!"

I have a story for you that will start our program. It's called, **"The Key Maker."**

© Youthlight, Inc.

The Key Maker

INTRODUCTION:

"Who can raise your hand and tell me what a key is?" (Discuss keys and what they do. Show a few keys) "Well, today we will start our Super Student Club with a story about a key maker.

I need everyone to listen with his/her eyes, ears and body. Show me that you are listening." (Wait until all students are sitting up, quiet, and their eyes are on you.)

Talon's Problem

LESSON 1

Once upon a time, because all good stories start once upon a time, a young eagle, named Talon wanted to be a winner in school. But, he didn't know how to be one and he didn't know anyone to ask.

"What do I need to know to be a good student in class?" asked Talon. Talon was supposed to start flying school in two weeks, and he needed to know quickly what to do in school to be super. He went to all his animal friends, but none seemed to know what Super Students do in school to make themselves winners.

Talon knew he needed to know the answers to these questions because flying is very important to an eagle, just like reading, math, and writing is important to boys and girls.

"Can you help Talon? What do good students do in school? How do they behave?"

*[Start a good discussion at this time.
Make sure the students talk one at a time.]*

© Youthlight, Inc.

Talon's Problem (cont.)

"Talon wanted to be ready for school, but who would show him the way? You have helped a lot. Next time we visit Talon, some other very special people will help him also. I wonder if they will use some of your ideas? We'll find out what happens the next time we visit Talon."

End of Session #1

K-1 LEADER'S GUIDE (CONT.)

Lesson 1 Questions

Ask these questions in your community circle at the end of session #1.

- What is a Super Student?
- Who is Talon?
- What is his problem?
- Why does he need to go to school?
- Why do we go to school?

Teachers/Leaders

At the end of the day send home the parent permission sheet for the Super Student Program. This is to inform the parents of your students about the Program and secure them as partners in this Program. (Please see the Black line Masters section at the end of this Grade K-1 section). Use the Kindergarten/First grade letter.

I'm Special

Using crayons, draw a picture of yourself with all the things that you love around you. Be ready to stand up when you are finished to talk about your picture. Distribute crayons and paper. When the students are finished get back into your community circle and discuss the pictures.

Role Playing the Lesson

Select a student to be Talon, the eagle. Pick four or five other students to be Talon's friends. See if they remember the story in Lesson 1. Try it over and over with other students

© Youthlight, Inc.

LESSON 2

The Club

Talon decided to ask his friends, Keith and Christina if they would help with his problem. He just had to find out how to be a good student in flying school. Keith and Christina lived in a cabin in the big woods with their parents. He knew they might be able to help him because they went to [Your school's name] school. Keith was a big 5th grader and Christina was in the 2nd grade. Talon flapped (as best as he could... He only crashed twice) to the cabin that overlooked a beautiful lake. Keith and Christina were playing in the woods near the cabin.

"Keith, Christina, can you help me?" asked Talon. The children looked up and saw the young eagle glide (not very gracefully) down from a small tree to a big log near the kids.

"What's up?" asked Christina. Talon knew Keith and Christina well. When Talon was just a baby eaglet, he had fallen out of his parent's nest and broke his wing. The children had taken him to Dr. Hardee, the veterinarian, who took care of all of their pets. Dr. Hardee had fixed Talon's wing and bandaged it. The children had had to feed and care for Talon because he could not fly back into his nest high in the biggest pine tree in the forest. Talon's mother had never been able to teach him how to fly.

Wild animals usually do not care for their young after the they have been handled by humans, so, the children had spent a lot of time in the woods with Talon. Talon had introduced them to many of the animals that lived nearby. In return, the kids had introduced Talon to Grinner, a flying squirrel for his first flying lesson. After the lesson, everyone agreed that Talon needed to learn better techniques and he needed a lot more practice.

LESSON 2

The Club (cont.)

"Keith and Christina, can you tell me what good students do so they can be winners in school? I'm starting flying school in two weeks, and I have to do well!" Talon said.

The children looked at each other in a puzzled way and then Keith said, " Well, you have to be good and listen."

The Club (cont.)

"Yes," said Christina, " and you have to do your work. Things like that."

"That will help," said Talon, " but there must be more." The kids thought. They loved their eagle friend and had had many good times with him during the summer. The more they thought the more they realized that they did not know what made a good student.

"Let's start a club! We can help each other become Super Students!" said Keith.

"A club?" asked Christina.

"Yes, a Super Student Club! We could have skills, membership cards, a pledge and rules for all Super Students to follow so they can be happy in school. Then, they will know how to be good students!" Keith said.

"Super!" said Christina and Talon together. "All students can join if they want to, and the three of us could be the first members."

Can you help the kids and Talon? Would you like to be in the Super Student Club? You can, you know! Would you like to be a Super Student? [Discuss why they might like to be in the Club and what they would have to do. Also, bring out the fact that they must believe that they can we winners in school.]

"Next time, we will learn more about the Super Student Club and the skills all great students use."

End of Session #2

K-1 LEADER'S GUIDE (CONT.)

Lesson 2 Questions

Ask these questions in your community circle at the end of session #2.

- What are the names of Talon's friends?
- What did Keith and Christina do for Talon when he was little?
- What was his problem?
- What was the Doctor's name? How did he help?
- Why did Talon not learn to fly when he was little?
- What was it that the kids decide to start? What is a club?

Role Playing the Lesson

Select characters for Talon, Keith, and Christina. See if the class remembers what dialogue took place at first. If you need to, re-read the beginning of Lesson 2 to start. Have the students act out the rest of the Lesson 2.

Meeting The Old Man

The children knew they needed help. How could they have a Super Student Club if they did not exactly know what good students do in school to be winners and make themselves happy?

"Let's ask the Key Maker," said Christina. "Of course," said Keith. "He is so wise and nice, and he'll surely know."

The Key Maker's home was deep in the forest, and the children knew the way. Talon stayed perched on Keith's shoulder as they trudged along to the Key Maker's home. "He will know," thought the children.

Soon they were at a beautiful little cottage in the big woods. It was a lovely setting with flowers all around the house. The group walked up a curved stone pathway to a beautiful large circular door with a huge iron knocker. Keith lifted the knocker and banged it up and down on the door.

The door creaked open and an old man with a friendly smile said, "Keith and Christina, good to see both of you! And who is your friend?"

"Oh, his name is Talon," said Christina.

"Well, come in children and bring your friend in also."

Talon hopped over to Keith's other shoulder as the children went into the beautiful little cottage. The cottage was so interesting inside. The children had been here many times before, but they always found that something new had been added. The Key Maker was always full of surprises. Fresh cut flowers were set on each table making the cottage look alive and colorful.

Meeting The Old Man (cont.)

All sort of keys were hanging on the walls from big ones to little ones. The keys shone brightly in many different colors as they picked up the light coming in through the windows. They gave the cottage a sparkling feeling of hope and excitement.

"Maybe here I can find my answers," thought Talon. "Come in and sit down," said the Key Maker, as he cleared a spot for

Meeting The Old Man (cont.)

the children on a large comfortable couch. "You must tell me what you are up to these days," said the old man with a smile on his face.

Keith spoke first, "Well, we would like to start a Super Student Club, but we don't know where to begin. We want to know what all good students do in school to be winners, so they can be happy!" said Christina.

"A Super Student Club," said the old man. "Well, you've come to the right place!"

The children and Talon smiled. The kids continued to talk. They knew Talon would not say anything, because he would only talk to the kids when they were alone in the woods. But, Talon was listening very carefully. They could see it in his sharp eyes.

"Where do we start?" Keith asked. "With these keys!" said the old man.

The Key Maker took out six large keys, each a different color, and laid them on the table in front of the children.

"These keys," said the old man, "will unlock the questions you have about Super Students. Each key will open a box that will have a lesson that a good student uses to be a winner in school."

"I knew he could help us!" said Christina. "But where are the boxes?"

The old man pointed to a large closet in front of the children. He opened the door of the closet, and six boxes each with a keyhole were neatly stacked on top of each other.

LESSON 3

Meeting The Old Man (cont.)

"Now, before we unlock the magic in the boxes, I must ask all of you the most important question. Are you ready?"

The kids looked at each other and then again at Talon. They all nodded their heads.

"What is it?" said Keith.

"Well," said the old man, "do you really believe you can be a winner in school? Do you want it that badly?"

The children looked again at each other and at Talon. Talon nodded and spread his wings.

Keith and Christina said together, "Yes, we do!"

"Good," said the Key Maker, "because the magic in the boxes will not work unless you believe you can be a winner."

End of Session #3

K-1 LEADER'S GUIDE (CONT.)

Lesson 3 Questions

Ask these questions in your community circle at the end of session #3.

- What is a key maker?
- How did he help the children and Talon?
- How could the children tell that Talon was listening carefully?
- What did the old man mean by saying, " You must believe that you can be a winner in school?"
- Describe the old man's house? What did it look like?
- Do you want to be winners in school? Why?

Have the students raise their hands. Count up the winners in your class. Say, " I see I have one [Jimmy], two [Jane], three [Sara] etc. They are making a commitment at this point. You could also have them stand as you count.

Teacher/ Leaders Says

In the next part of our story we will start opening the boxes with the magic keys. That will be exciting, won't it? What do you think they will find in the boxes that will make them Super Students? We'll find out next time we meet.

Role Playing the Lesson

Pick students for the characters: Talon, Keith, Christina, and the Key Maker. Act out the lesson. If you need to re-read parts of Lesson 3, please do.

Draw the Key Maker's cottage

Hand out a white sheet of drawing paper and re-read the section of this lesson that describes the inside of the Key Maker's home. Have the children draw the picture that comes to mind as you read this section.

READ THIS SECTION:
Talon hopped over to Keith's other shoulder as the children went into the beautiful little cottage. The cottage was so interesting inside. The children had been here many times before, but they always found that something new had been added. The Key Maker was always full of surprises. Fresh cut flowers were set on each table making the cottage look alive and colorful. Many kinds of keys were hanging on the walls from big ones to little ones. The keys shone brightly in many different colors as they picked up the light coming in through the windows. They gave the cottage a sparkling feeling of hope and excitement.

The White Key

"Well, are we ready?" said the Key Maker.

"Here is the first key." The first key was white and heavy. Keith took it and stuck it into the keyhole for box number one and turned it. The lock opened and Keith pulled up the lid.

Inside the box was a white note that said, **"I WILL LISTEN, OBEY, AND TRUST MY TEACHER."**

The White Key (cont.)

"This is the first and most important rule to follow in order to be a Super Student," the old man said. "It is the most important thing a good student does every day in school. Your teacher cares for you and wants you to be happy and healthy. Good students listen the first time their teacher tells them to do something. Are you a good listener?

Good students obey and do everything their teacher tells them to do. Do you obey? Trusting your teacher means believing your teacher will take care of you and teach you the things that you need to know. Do you trust your teacher?"

The Key maker continued, "Without your teachers, you would be lost in school. You would not be able to learn to read, to write or to do math. You need your teachers so… much, and the way you say thank you to them is to listen, obey, and trust them every day. All of the other five skills to be a Super Student come from this first one." Keith, Christina, and Talon all nodded in approval.

The Key Maker continued, "We come to school to learn from the teacher. That's why we listen. If we don't listen, we don't learn. If we don't learn, we don't grow. We need our teachers if we are going to be happy in school. Do you care for and trust your teacher? Have you told her/him that you do? Can you do it now?"

End of Session #4

K-1 LEADER'S GUIDE (CONT.)

Lesson 4 Questions

Ask these questions in your community circle at the end of session #4.

- What was the color of the first key?
- What did the first key unlock?
- What does 'listen to your teacher' mean? How does it help you to learn?
- Why is it important to listen to the teacher?
- Who is showing me that you are listening now?
- How do I know that you are listening to me?
- Suppose, you do not want to listen to the teacher? What would happen?
- What should you do to be a good listener?

Color the Keys

Distribute the Color the Keys worksheet (see Black line Masters at the end of this story). Have the students put their name at the top and outline the first white key in black crayon. Talk about the white key and its significance. Make a folder and keep this sheet of paper in the student's Super Student Folder. You will use this sheet again and again as we work through skills and the colored keys.

Trace the Skill and Symbol

Distribute the Trace the Skill worksheet (see Black line Masters at the end of this story). Have the students trace the letters of the first skill and the symbol. The symbol will help them to learn the words of the skill. Have the students then cut out the Skill and paste it on a clean sheet of paper with their name on it. Keep this paper in your Super Student Folder so the skills can be added as the lessons grow. Be sure to send this home when all the skills are traced and pasted.

© Youthlight, Inc.

The Yellow Key

Christina picked up the second key. It was bright yellow. She gently placed the key into the keyhole of the second box.

"It fits!" Christina said as she turned the key. The lid opened, and Christina picked out a yellow note that read, **"I WILL RAISE MY HAND TO SPEAK."**

"Wow," said Christina. "Now we are getting down to what a Super Student does to show he/she is Super."

The Yellow Key (cont.)

"Yes," said the old man. "This skill is very important. All Super Students do it every day. In school, boys and girls are in a room with lots of other students. If everyone talks at the same time, no one can hear. Also, it is good manners to speak one at a time.

The teacher controls the discussion in the classroom, so we must keep our eyes on the teacher when we are in a group and she/he is leading us. It is the teacher's job to lead us when we are in a group, so we need to wait for the teacher to ask the questions and then raise our hands to answer.

If you have a question, you can raise your hand so your teacher will see you. When she calls your name, then you can ask your question. Super Students know this rule and use it all the time in class. They know that taking turns is important in school. It shows that you have manners and respect."

"I understand!" said Christina. " One rule builds on the next one. I need to listen, obey, and trust my teacher. Then, using the next rule helps me to show that I am a good listener when I raise my hand in class." Talon flapped his wings in approval.

"That's good," said the Key Maker. "Do you raise your hand in class when you want to speak?"

End of Session #5

K-1 LEADER'S GUIDE (CONT.)

Lesson 5 Questions

Discuss skill #2-- I WILL RAISE MY HAND

Make sure the students are raising their hands to answer these questions. You could say, " I only pick Super Students who raise their hands." or," I need you to raise your hand to answer this question."

Ask these questions in your community circle at the end of session #2.

- What was the color of the second key?
- What did the second key open? What was the rule?
- Why should we raise our hands in class?
- What did the old man mean when he said, "It is good manners to raise your hand in class?"
- Why is taking turns to talk so important in class?
- If everyone talked at the same time, what would happen?
- What is respect?

Color the Keys

Distribute the Color the Keys worksheet from the Super Student Folder you have created. Have the students color the second key yellow. Keep this worksheet and continue to color these keys as each lesson continues to unlock the Super Student Skills. Be sure to send this home when all the keys are finished.

Trace the Skill and Symbol

Distribute the Trace the Skill worksheet from the Super Student Folder you have created. Have the students trace the letters of the second skill and the symbol. The symbol will help them to learn the words of the skill. Have the students then cut out the skill and paste it on the sheet of paper with the first skill. Keep this paper so the skills can be added as the lessons grow. Be sure to send this home when all the skills are traced and pasted.

The Green Key

The third key was green. Keith started to lift it, but it was too heavy.

"Can you help me, Christina?" he asked. Christina grabbed the key, but to their surprise, they could not lift it to the keyhole.

"I'm sorry kids, but I can't help you," said the Key Maker. " It will break the magic. Do your best and don't give up."

Talon hopped on to the table, and with Keith on one end and Christina on the other end, Talon grabbed the key in the middle with his strong beak.

The Green Key (cont.)

"One, two, three," said Keith. With a great effort the three managed to place the key to the third box's keyhole.

"Whew," said Christina. "That was tough."

"Yes, but all of you worked together and you did your best. That's why you made it to the keyhole. You didn't quit!" said the old man.

The children and Talon turned the key and the lid opened. The note in the box was written in big green letters. It read, **"I WILL GIVE MY BEST."**

"Do you see what I mean," said the old man. "This is rule number three. It is very important just like the others. Remember your problem lifting the key? All three of you gave your best to open the lock and you succeeded. Super Students work hard in school and do their best every time they have something to do. They push themselves to do their very best work. They keep trying and trying. Being lazy is not for a Super Student. When Super Students start to feel lazy, they push themselves forward to finish the job."

"Just like we did with the key!" said Christina.

"Exactly!" said the Key Maker. "All of you gave your best!"

End of Session #6

K-1 LEADER'S GUIDE (CONT.)

Lesson 6 Questions

Ask these questions in your community circle at the end of the session #6.

- What was the color of the third key?
- How did the kids get the key up to the keyhole?
- What would have happened if the children and Talon had not given their best?
- What does 'giving your best' mean?
- Why should you give your best in school?
- Who can tell about a time today that you gave your best in school?
- Can you be a Super Student if you quit when the work gets hard? Why?
- What happens when you try hard with all your work in school?

Color the Keys

Distribute the Color the Keys worksheet from the Super Student Folder you have created. Have the students color the third key green. Keep this worksheet and continue to color these keys as each lesson continues to unlock the Super Student Skills. Be sure to send this home when all the keys are finished.

Trace the Skill and Symbol

Distribute the Trace the Skill worksheet from the Super Student Folder you have created. Have the students trace the letters of the third skill and the symbol. The symbol will help them to learn the words of the skill. Have the students then cut out the skill and paste it on the sheet of paper with the first and second skill. Keep this paper so the skills can be added as the lessons grow. Be sure to send this home when all the skills are traced and pasted.

© Youthlight, Inc.

The Red Key

The children and Talon had learned so much! The Key Maker had given them answers to what a Super Student does to be good. They were feeling that the Super Student Club was going to happen.

The fourth key was red. Keith grabbed the key. It was very light and easy to pick up. He placed it in the keyhole and started to turn it, but before he finished turning the key, he noticed some writing on the box just above the keyhole.

I WILL FINISH ALL MY WORK

The Red Key (cont.)

"Can you read the writing, Christina?" Christina leaned over and said, "Beat the work, and don't let the work beat you!"

"What does it mean?" asked Christina.

"Let's find out," said the Key Maker. "Open the box."

Keith finished turning the key and the box opened. Inside the box the note said, **"I WILL FINISH ALL MY WORK."**

The Key Maker said, "This is the fourth rule all good students obey to be Super."

"Does it mean homework?" asked Keith.

"Yes, it does. It means your classroom work, your homework, and all of the other jobs that your teacher gives you to do. Do you understand? You beat the work! Don't let the work beat you! You finish your work. If you don't understand the work, and it is hard to finish, it is your job to ask your teacher for help. Don't keep it deep inside, but ask for help," said the old man.

"And use rule number two — **I WILL RAISE MY HAND** for help!" said Christina.

"That's right!" the Key Maker said. "Super Students seek out help. They look for people to help them if they are having a problem."

"Just like seeing your school counselor," said Keith.

"That's correct!" said the Key Maker. "Help is all around you. People want you to be a winner in school, but you have to want it also. So, ask for help, then give your best and finish all your work."

End of session #7

K-1 LEADER'S GUIDE (CONT.)

Lesson 7 Questions

Ask these questions in your community circle at the end of session #7.

- What was the color of this key?
- Who can give me some examples of some of the work I give you in class to finish?
- Why do I give you this work?
- What does finishing your entire work mean?
- What does 'beat the work' mean?
- Why is it important?
- What happens when you do not finish your work?
- When you don't understand the work I give you to finish, what should you do?

Color the Keys

Distribute the Color the Keys worksheet from the Super Student Folder you have created. Have the students color the fourth key red. Keep this worksheet and continue to color these keys as each lesson continues to unlock the Super Student Skills. Be sure to send this home when all the keys are finished.

Trace the Skill and Symbol

Distribute the Trace the Skill worksheet from the Super Student Folder you have created. Have the students trace the letters of the fourth skill and the symbol. The symbol will help them to learn the words of the skill. Have the students then cut out the skill and paste it on the sheet of paper with the first, second and third skill. Keep this paper so the skills can be added as the lessons grow. Be sure to send this home when all the skills are traced and pasted.

© Youthlight, Inc.

The Blue Key

Keith, Christina, and Talon looked at the next key. They had not noticed this before, but this key was strange. It was changing into different shades of blue as they stared at it. First, it was light blue, then darker blue, then it was a deep, dark blue. It then would turn back to light blue and repeat the color changes.

"Strange!" said Christina. "Yeah, weird," said Keith. "Why is it changing, Key Maker?"

"Because, it is trying to get our attention. If you do not use the next rule, you will be sad and blue. All Super Students use this skill, so they can be great students."

"What is it?" said Christina.
"Let's see," said the old man.

Christina grabbed the key and when she lifted it she felt happy and wanted to smile.

"What's making you smile?" asked Keith.

"You'll see. It will make you happy to know this rule," said the Key Maker.

Christina placed the key in the keyhole and turned the key. She pulled up the lid and grabbed the note. It read, in blue ink, **"I WILL WORK OUT PROBLEMS WITH OTHERS."**

"What does it mean," asked Christina? *(Does anyone here in our class know what it means? Let's see what the Key Maker says.)*

"It means that when you go to school there are other boys and girls in class. School is not only for you but also for lots of children. You

The Blue Key (cont.)

must learn to live with them and be happy. You cannot have your own way all the time.

If you have a problem with another student, you need to talk it out. If that student will not share or listen, ask your teacher to help.

Some students will try to lead you into trouble by getting you so mad that you lose your cool, and you say and do things that place you into trouble."

"You mean like a fight?" asked Christina.

 # The Blue Key (cont.)

"Yes, a fight where you push, hit, or kick someone. Super Students know that fighting is not allowed in school. So when you start fighting, even if you are hit first, you will be trouble along with the other student."

"Our teacher says, two wrongs don't make a right!" said Keith.

"That's correct!" said the old man. " When two students do something wrong, they are both wrong. Fighting, hitting, kicking or saying hurtful words are not things that will help you. It will get you into trouble and take away all of the good Super Student feelings that you have been working on."

"What should we do if someone hits us first," asked Christina?

"Good question! Say, 'No, I won't fight!' Then, move away and tell your teacher. When you have problems with others, and you will have them, it is best to try to work it out by talking to that student. If that doesn't work, ask the teacher or your counselor to help. They love children and are trained to help boys and girls through problems."

The Key Maker continued, "School is a good place to work on problems. Teachers, counselors or principals are not going to let you get hurt. So, let them know what's going on. Talk to them about your problems. That's what Super Students do. That's why they're winners!"

End of Session #8

K-1 LEADER'S GUIDE (CONT.)

Lesson 8 Questions

Ask these questions in your community circle at the end of session #8.

- What was the color of this key?
- Why was it changing colors? What did the old man say?
- Why should we work out problems with others?
- What usually happens when we don't talk it out when we have a problem with another student?
- Why should we come to the teacher when we have a problem that we can't work out?
- Why do both students who fight find themselves in trouble?
- What did the old man mean when he said, "You will be blue if you don't follow this rule!"
- Why is fighting wrong?

Color the Keys

Distribute the Color the Keys worksheet from the Super Student Folder you have created. Have the students color the fifth key blue. Keep this worksheet and continue to color these keys as each lesson continues to unlock the Super Student Skills. Be sure to send this home when all the keys are finished.

Trace the Skill and Symbol

Distribute the Trace the Skill worksheet from the Super Student Folder you have created. Have the students trace the letters of the fifth skill and the symbol. The symbol will help them to learn the words of the skill. Have the students then cut out the skill and paste it on the sheet of paper with the first, second, third, fourth skill. Keep this paper so the skills can be added as the lessons grow. Be sure to send this home when all the skills are traced and pasted.

The Black Key

The last key was a beautiful shiny black color. The children, Talon, and the Key Maker looked at the last key with a little sadness in their eyes. They had learned so much from the Key Maker. They could start their Super Student Club now! They had the skills and rules they needed. They knew the way. Also, they knew that Talon would now have the skills to help him in flying school.

The Key Maker had taken them through white, yellow, green, red, blue and now black magic keys. Each magic key had opened up a skill or rule that all good Super Students use to win in school. No one had ever taught them these things before.

Of course, they had never asked the question, "What do all good students do to be super in school?" until now. They loved the old Key Maker. He had always been so kind and given such good advice, but it was getting late and they would have to return home shortly. So, they hesitated a little as Keith picked up the last beautiful black magic key, and placed it into the keyhole, and turned the key.

As the lid opened, the Key Maker said, "If you really want to be a winner in school, you can do it! If you use the skills, good things will happen to you!"

The note read, **"I WILL HAVE A POSITIVE, HEALTHY ATTITUDE!"**

"Do you know what a good attitude means?" asked the old man.

"Tell us," said Christina.

"Well, your attitude is the way you feel about things. Your attitude is the only thing you can control in your life. You can choose to be happy or sad, helpful or hurtful. You are the boss over your body

LESSON 9 — The Black Key (cont.)

and your mind. You decide what you say and do in every situation. If you decide to be a winner in school, a Super Student, you will use these skills I have shared with you with the magic keys. If you will use these skills, good things will happen to you."

He continued, "If you will use these skills, it will show others that you are winning in school. Your attitude reflects if you are a hard worker or a quitter. It shows if you have manners and respect or if you are selfish and spoiled."

The Key Maker said, "You can't blame anyone else if you don't have a good attitude. You can take full credit for it yourself. A positive, healthy attitude is a great thing to have to work you through any problem or situation. Everyone can tell if you have a good attitude by the way you talk and act. It shows in your smiling face. So, put on a positive, healthy attitude and use all of the Super Student Skills that you have unlocked and good things will happen to you. That's a promise!"

End of session # 9

K-1 LEADER'S GUIDE (CONT.)

Lesson 9 Questions

Ask these questions in your community circle at the end of session #9.

- What was the color of this key?
- What was this Super Student skill?
- What does attitude mean?
- How can you tell if your attitude is good?
- What kind of a listener will you be?
- How many of you want to join Talon and his friends in the Super Student Club?

Color the Keys

Distribute the Color the Keys worksheet from the Super Student Folder you have created. Have the students color the sixth key black. Once all the keys are finished, send this home with the parent permission slip, membership card, and certificate for the Super Student Club.

Trace the Skill and Symbol

Distribute the Trace the Skill worksheet from the Super Student Folder you have created. Have the students trace the letters of the sixth skill and the symbol. The symbol will help them to learn the words of the skill. Have the students then cut out the skill and paste it on the sheet of paper with the first, second, third, fourth, and fifth skill. Keep this sheet so the skills can be added as the lessons grow. Be sure to send this paper home after the tenth lesson with the parent permission slip, membership card, and certificate for the Super Student Club.

The Pledge

With that, the Key Maker gave them all a big smile and a hug. "I have something for you and your Super Student Club members," said the old man.

He opened a beautiful wooden chest that was near the table. On the top of the chest were the words, "Survival Kit." He reached in, and pulled out three rolled up papers and handed them to the three guests.

"Read it, Keith." He said.

Keith unrolled the paper and began to read:

"My attitude is the only thing I can control. I can choose to be happy or sad, helpful or hurtful. I can choose to be a winner in school.

LESSON 10

The Pledge (cont.)

"This can be our pledge!" said Keith.

"It would make me very happy if you would use it," said the Key Maker.

"Great!" Christina said. "Then, we have all we need to start the club!"

Talon smiled, and all could see that he was very happy.

"All you need now is the other students to join to be Super Students. They will need to be able to follow the rules," said the Key Maker.

"Oh, we'll have the students! Everyone will want to sign up! It's fun to be good in school!" said Keith.

As the children and Talon left the cottage, the sun was setting. It was a beautiful ending to a special day. The three friends slowly walked back through the forest to the children's cabin in the big woods.

As they walked along, Talon told the kids that he was going to use all the skills in his flying school classes. He would remember all the great ideas that the old man had shared with them on this special day. And, of course, he had the pledge.

"Do you think that the students in the other classes in our school will join the Super Student Club?" asked Christina as they walked down the hill to the cabin.

"I hope so," said Keith. "Let's ask them!"

End of session # 10

© Youthlight, Inc.

GRADES K-1 LEADER'S GUIDE (CONT.)

Lesson 10 Questions

Ask these questions in your community circle at the end of session #10.

- What was the present the Key Maker gave the kids and Talon?
- What is a pledge? (a promise)
- What is a promise?
- What did the Key Maker promise the kids and Talon?
- Did you like the Key Maker? Why?
- Do you think a lot of kids will want to be Super Students?

Teacher/Leader, you will need the Take the Pledge Commitment Sheet located at end of this K-1 Program in the Black line Master Section for Grades K-1.

Ask Your Class:

Who would like to sign up for our Super Student Club? Do you believe that you can be super? Can you follow the Super Student Skills and promise to keep trying even if you have a problem once in a while?

Let's sign up today! I'm going to have you sign up on this sheet of paper. Put your name on this paper. If you have problems putting your name on the paper, I will help you. (This is the Take the Pledge Commitment Sheet)

You will need to learn, memorize and do all of the skills that the Key Maker talked about. Can you do that? Of course, you can! I know you can all be winners in school!

Teacher/ Leaders:

Distribute the Super Student Membership Cards, Certificates, Focus Skills, and Pledge as a Packet to go home. (See the Black line Masters at the end of this section for Grades K-1).

Make sure you copy the Super Student Focus Sheet and My Pledge for the students to have at their desks or tape them on the wall to refer to. Because kindergarten/first graders are learning to read, the Focus Skill Sheet for your level has symbols for each skill. This will be a great help for you to reference during the school day. For example, if a student is not listening to you during a lesson, you can point to the symbol of the ear on his skill sheet.

It is vital to get the parents involved at some point during the year to continue to invigorate the Super Student Club and the concepts you have just introduced. After the first marking period that your Super Student Program is functioning, try having your students memorize the Focus Skills and the Pledge. This memorization activity will be very important for the rest of the year and for the next year's Super Student Program in the next grade (Use Black line Master at the end of the Grade K-1 section). Reward the students who memorize the Super Student Focus Skills and My Pledge. Make a big deal out of being a good student!

K-1 LEADER'S GUIDE (CONT.)

Teacher/Leaders: You will need to reinforce the Super Student Focus Skills and My Pledge each week in community circle by going over the Skills and having your children memorize the pledge. This is your Super Student Club meeting time during your community circle. Keep the Focus Skills and My Pledge displayed in the room. As their reading gets better and better they will read the skills and pledge for themselves. In the mean time, use the symbols to help your children know what Focus Skill you are referring to.

Send home the prepared letter for memorization to the parents. This will include them as partners to help their children memorize the Super Student Focus Skills and My Pledge. With their parents' help, the children can memorize the skills and the pledge. I highly recommended that they do this. Point out during the week who is doing which skill and how happy you are about their progress as Super Students.

The Awards Celebration It is very important to celebrate students and their school efforts and achievements. I recommend that you celebrate your students at each report card period. During this celebration ceremony, they can be rewarded with medals, trophies, or certificates. Or better yet, celebrate them every interim period of your report card period. Start today and make a big deal out of being a Super Student!

Counselors: This Program allows you to wire a whole school for celebrating excellence and achievement grade by grade. Research has proven that effective schools focus on student effort and recognition of achievement (Marzano, 2001). As you spearhead the Super Student Program and direct the reward and recognition program, you will be having a major impact on your school that is measurable and effective. It will fit into any goals based guidance program for the elementary schools. If you have the use of a TV studio in your school, your follow up in classes and on TV will be very supportive to your teachers and staff. You can coordinate this program throughout the school or use the stories in your developmental guidance lessons in individual classrooms.

© Youthlight, Inc.

THE *SUPER STUDENT* CLUB PACKET FOR K-1

A tool is only good if you use it. The Super Student Program will only help you in the classroom if you use the concepts and skills. It is a tool, a survival kit, for you and your children. As you refer to the skills when you see them being used by your children, the students will respond and work harder for you. They will become the Super Students that you want. Be patient and persistent. After a while, these skills will become a habit and a way for your students to be successful in school. It will serve them not only with you this year but in future grades. In addition, it will become something that they will use as they progress into the world of work.

After the student signs the commitment sheet, his/her packet includes; the Super Student Focus Skills Sheet, the pledge, membership card and certificate. Many teachers place the Super Student Focus Skills Sheet and My Pledge right on the student's desk or on a bulletin board with each child's membership cards. Keeping the Super Student Focus Skills nearby allows you to visit the concepts during the day, if needed.

Teachers, many times, will take pictures with the students holding the membership cards. They will display the pictures where all visitors can see them. Teachers, send home the parent letters (see the Black line masters). In any case, it is important to display and continue to work with the concepts and skills during the community circle or group time throughout the year.

If you start the program at the beginning of the school year, I suggest that you have a mid-year contest for memorizing the Super Student Focus Skills and My Pledge. Enclosed in the Black line masters is a sample letter to the parents for this memorization challenge.

The more you celebrate your Super Students and draw attention to the Focus Skills and the Super Student Club the more your students will improve their Super Student behavior. I cannot stress enough this vital repetition to develop the skills so that they are habitual. Young children love this repetition, so don't think they will become bored.

The use of The Super Student Focus Skills Checklist (a Black line master) is highly recommended to get ready for the Awards Celebration. Have your students use this checklist at least twice a week to keep tabs on their attitude and behavior before the marking period is over. This checklist is very useful for arrangements that you have with parents on daily reports that need to go home concerning their student's behavior. This checklist is an excellent form to monitor your Super Student Club members before the Awards Celebration. Please use any of the worksheet exercises in the Black line masters to bring your students the needed reminder for using the skills on a daily basis.

The parent information should go home. You will need to continue to secure the parent's cooperation for the program throughout the year. Remember to celebrate the winners at each report card time. These are students who are using most of the skills on a regular basis. Look at the skills with them. Are they listening, raising their hand, being prepared for their work, giving their best, finishing their work, working out problems with others, and demonstrating a positive healthy attitude in class? If so, they need to be celebrated.

Our school calls this a Renaissance Celebration, and we do it four times a year school-wide. I cannot stress using this celebration and recognition every nine week enough. It is vital that your school celebrates at least four times a year the product you are producing, namely, students.

If your school has not adopted the Super Student Program school-wide, you can do this celebration in your classroom after report cards are given out. Invite the parents of the winners to the celebration. Encourage picture taking and serve refreshments. Celebrate your students!

The SUPER STUDENT Program

Reproducible Blackline Masters for grades K-1

© Youthlight, Inc.

SUPER STUDENT CLUB MEMBERSHIP

Dear Parents of Kindergarten and First Grade Students,

We are beginning a special program, called the Super Student Club at our school. This program will reinforce our instruction and achievement on a daily basis.

We need your help!
The Super Student Club was developed to help students:
- Take responsibility for their learning.
- Learn a systemic model for improving their schoolwork.
- Improve their effort toward academic tasks.
- Absorb basic study skills and concepts that improve the effectiveness and efficiency of their learning.
- Enhance self-esteem.
- Develop lifelong learners with positive healthy attitudes.

How can you help?
Please go over the Focus Skills and My Pledge with your child. He/she will have to learn and do these skills every day. Please support your child's teacher and sign this permission slip so they can join the Super Student Club. We believe that any student can be a Super Student. It is all about a super attitude! Please call us at the school if you have any questions.

★ Super Student Focus Skills
1. I will listen, obey, and trust my teacher.
2. I will raise my hand to speak.
3. I will give my best.
4. I will finish my work.
5. I will work out problems with others.
6. I will have a positive, healthy attitude.

★ My Pledge
My attitude is the only thing I can control in life.
I can choose to be happy or sad, helpful or hurtful.
I can choose to be a winner in school.

I give permission for my child to be in the Super Student Club. I will support the program. I will go over the Focus Skills and My Pledge with my child and keep in touch with his/her teacher throughout the year.

Child's name _____

Teacher _____ Grade _____

Parent Signature _____

Color The Keys.

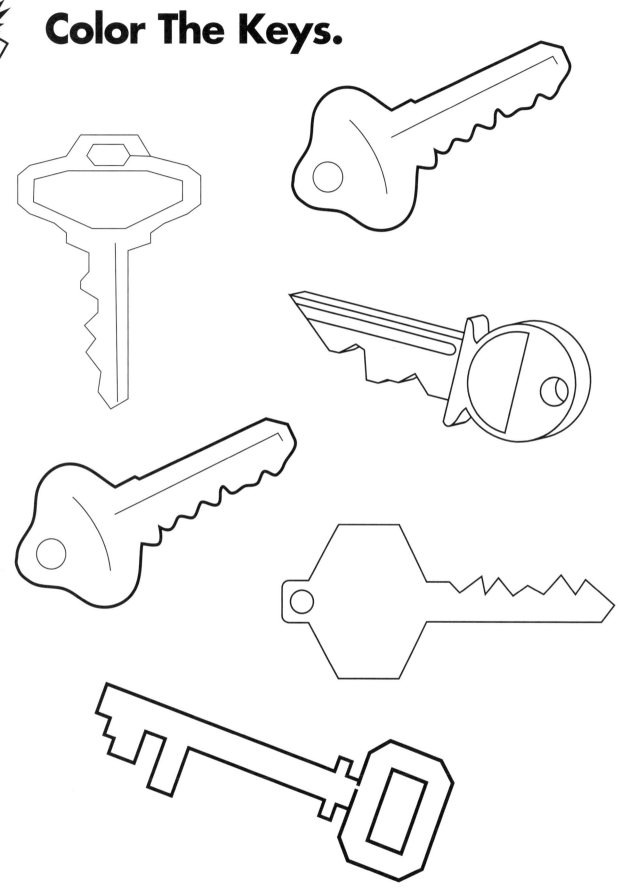

Trace the skill and symbol.

1. I will listen, obey, and trust my teacher.
   _____

2. I will raise my hand to speak.
   _____

3. I will give my best.
   _____

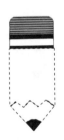
4. I will finish all my work.
   _____

5. I will work out problems with others.
   _____

6. I will have a positive, healthy attitude.
   _____

TAKE THE PLEDGE!

My Pledge

My attitude is the only thing I can control in life.

I can choose to be happy or sad, helpful or hurtful.

I can choose to be a winner in school.

I am signing this commitment sheet with my classmates and accepting my membership card for the Super Student Club. By signing this commitment sheet, I am saying that I want to be a Super Student and will use the Super Student Focus Skills everyday. My teacher has the right and responsibility to correct me when I stray from the Focus Skills and Pledge. I will also say the Pledge and abide by this Super Student Code. My teacher believes that I can be a Super Student. If I believe that I can, it will happen, with hard work!

Signed:_____ Date: _____

Teacher_____ Grade _____

★ COMMITMENT SHEET

© Youthlight, Inc.

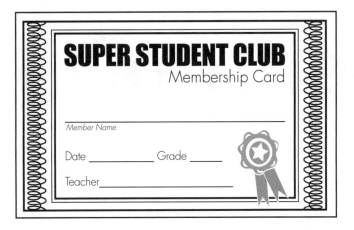
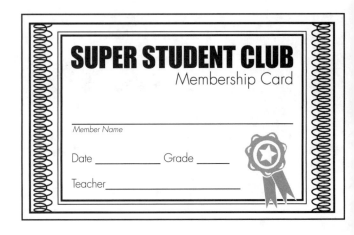

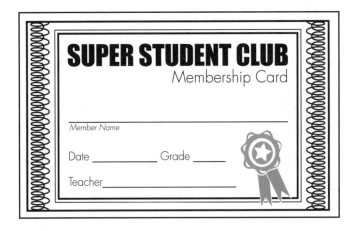

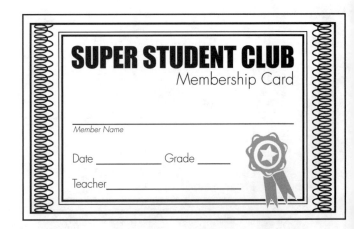

SUPER STUDENT
Certificate

This certifies that

_____

Has used the Focus Skills in class, has taken the Super Student Pledge, and is officially in the Super Student Club.

_____ _____
Teacher   Date

© Youthlight, Inc.

★ FOCUS SKILLS ★

 1. I will listen, obey, and trust my teacher.

 2. I will raise my hand to speak.

 3. I will give my best.

 4. I will finish all my work.

 5. I will work out problems with others.

 6. I will have a positive, healthy attitude.

My Pledge

My attitude is the only thing I can control in life.

I can choose to be happy or sad, helpful or hurtful.

I can choose to be a winner in school.

★ SUPER STUDENT FOCUS SKILLS & PLEDGE MEMORIZATION

Dear Parents of Kindergarten and First Grade Students,

We need your help!
As you know, we have started the most important club your child can be part of at our school . . . The Super Student Club! This special program reinforces our instruction and achievement on a daily basis. The Super Student Club was developed so we could remind students daily about the skills that make winners in school. As you are aware, the Super Student Club has Focus Skills and My Pledge that we would like students to memorize. Could you please help your child to learn all the skills and the pledge? We feel it is very important that the students learn the skills and make the pledge a part of their student life.

How can you help?
Please go over the Focus Skills and the Pledge with your child. He/she will have to learn and do these skills every day. Please support your child's teacher and sign this permission slip so they can join the Super Student Club. We believe that any student can be a Super Student. It is all about a super attitude! Please call us at the school if you have any questions.

★ Super Student Focus Skills
1. I will listen, obey, and trust my teacher.
2. I will raise my hand to speak.
3. I will give my best.
4. I will finish my work.
5. I will work out problems with others.
6. I will have a positive, healthy attitude.

★ My Pledge
My attitude is the only thing I can control in life.
I can choose to be happy or sad, helpful or hurtful.
I can choose to be a winner in school.

How can you help?
Please go over the Focus Skills and My Pledge with your child. Have them memorize the skills and the pledge. Please support your child's teacher and sign this pledge to memorize.

RETURN TO TEACHER
I promise to teach the Super Student Focus Skills and My Pledge to my children and will see that he/she memorizes these important facts.

Student's name_____

Teacher_____ Grade_____

Parent/Guardian Signature_____

© Youthlight, Inc.

SUPER STUDENT FOCUS SKILLS CHECKLIST

Are you doing these skills today?

Place a smiley face in front of each skill that you did all day long.

Today is _____

Super Student _____

Teacher _____ Grade _____

_____   I did listen, obey, and trust my teacher.

_____   I did raise my hand to speak.

_____   I did give my best.

_____   I did finish all my work.

_____   I did work out problems with others.

_____   I did have a positive, healthy attitude.

How many smiley faces did you get today? _____
Teacher Comments:

Parent signature_____

The Super Student Program
LEADER'S GUIDE FOR GRADES 2-3

Rationale

The second and third grades are exciting and productive years in elementary school. Most of the students can read, write, and do basic math. They have verbal skills and are starting to understand that school is a system with rules and work requirements. They are practicing social relationships now and are starting to become more independent and responsible. Many students are now aware if they are winning or not at school. Some may have been retained by now and some are involved in special education.

If this is the first year of The Super Student Program for your school, the students in your class would have never heard of the phrase, 'winning in school' or of the survival skills that all Super Students use. In other words, this program is new to them and to you. If your school adopts the program, it will make the years that follow much easier because the students will have experienced the concepts and skills in the previous grades. Each year after the first, it will be that much easier because everyone will have been exposed to the concepts and will be speaking the same language. Hopefully, by that time, your recognition awards program will be in sync with the Super Student Club. After three to four years, the Super Student Program will give you some serious academic advantages in your school.

Regardless, as you start your year with your class, believe that they are yours to mold. Some students will probably have bad habits, but they will follow your lead as you begin the year with the program.

While great learning does not always occur in group activities, good educators will, at times, pull large or small groups together to introduce or build on a concept. This is the teachable moment for Super Student behavior. Nurture the Super Student skills and they grow. Celebrate them and they remain. These skills will become the survival tool kit for your students as they progress through the grades. They will become habitual for most students. So, while computer programs will be helpful and individual projects and exploration will be profitable, group learning and sharing will be the special time when self-esteem grows and learning from and with others begins.

The definition of a Super Student is not to have all knowledge. To be able to take instruction and direction, to be able to solve problems, to be respectful, to give one's best is what defines a great student. To be able to work out problems with others, ask appropriate questions, and most importantly, to posses a positive, healthy attitude, these are the skills that will produce Super Students that are winners in school and who are lifelong learners and achievers. Basically, it's quite a simple definition. It is all about a super attitude!

I believe that true education brings young students from irresponsible to responsible, from immature to mature, from selfish to unselfish, and from ignorant to knowledgeable. Students need to know how to survive in a group and how to win in a school setting. The skills identified in the Super Student Program are the skills that all winners use in school to make school the most profitable experience possible.

© Youthlight, Inc.

GRADES 2-3 LEADER'S GUIDE (CONT.)

Getting Started

Now you are ready to start the story and lessons that will lead your students to join the Super Student Club. The preparation for the Program for the students takes only fifteen to twenty minutes twice a week for five weeks. All of this is done during your community circle or shared reading time. The story is engaging and interesting. At the end of each story/lesson are appropriate questions and activities to further develop your students into Super Students. The story contains all the work you would normally do during a shared reading time or language arts period with your students. Teachers consider it part of their reading program. So, you are doing academics while you are working with the Super Student Program!

Story: TALON and the MAGIC EGGS

Use this story for grades 2 and 3. It will be read to students in a group setting. The story is reproducible. You may, of course, copy the text and have the children read along with you or let them read it taking turns in your group. A copy would be an advantage for any student who is absent or a student who would need to revisit the story in the future. It would be best, if they sit on a carpet or floor in front of you. A community circle and family atmosphere is recommended. Of course, discuss any of the illustrations as they apply to the story.

Introduction

TEACHER/LEADER SAYS:

"Today class, we will be starting an adventure. I am starting a Super Student Club and would like everyone to join! Our club will do exciting projects and each one of its members will learn how to win and be happy in school.

I will teach anyone who wants to be a Super Student the skills necessary to win in school. My problem is that I can't make you join. I would like everyone to be in the club, but I can't make you be in it. It is a choice you will have to make for yourself.

I would like to tell you about the club and what a Super Student is. Then, after you have heard all about the program, I will invite you to sign up to be a member. Would you like to hear more about our club and what you have to do to be a member? Good! Let's start!"

I have a story for you that will start our program. It's called, **"Talon and the Magic Eggs."**

Talon and the Magic Eggs

The Project
LESSON 1

Daniel and Cheryl were looking for a project. The students attended Green Sea Floyds Elementary School in Horry County, SC. Daniel was in the fifth grade and Cheryl was in the second grade.

They were getting bored when they turned off the TV and ran outside to climb up into their tree house to talk.

"You know, Daniel," said Cheryl. "I just want to do something helpful and exciting! I'm tired of TV and playing video games."

"Yeah, same old thing! Let's try to think of something we can do to liven things up! Maybe we could help in school. I can ask Mrs. Quick if she has a project we could help her with."

"Mrs. Quick was saying yesterday that she wished that more students would be good students." Cheryl said. "She was worried that they were wasting their time and not winning in school."

"Yes, the Celebration Program is starting and all the teachers want as many students as possible to win Gold, Silver, and Bronze awards. Maybe we could start a club and hold meetings in our tree house. We could practice being good students and try to have as many students as possible to join our group. Then, they could go to school and be winners in school. They could win the Celebration Awards," said Daniel.

"Great! That would be super!" said Cheryl.

"What did you say, Cheryl?"

"I said, 'That would be super'."

The Project (cont.)

"I've an idea! Let's call it the Super Student Club!" said Daniel.

"Super Student Club!" replied Cheryl, "Sounds Great! Let's get started."

The next day in school, after they told Mrs. Quick about the idea for the club, the children started to make posters. Mrs. Quick was so impressed that she asked them to share it with the principal, Mrs. Huggins.

The Project (cont.)

"I think this is great! What will you teach the club members?" Mrs. Huggins asked.

"We'll teach them to be Super Students in school so they can win the Celebration Awards," said Cheryl.

"What are the skills they will learn to be a Super Student?" asked Mrs. Huggins.

Cheryl looked at Daniel with the question in her eyes. Daniel replied, "We'll just have to go to the tree house to figure it out."

"That sounds great," replied Mrs. Huggins. "Good luck and let me know when you have some ideas."

After school the children ran home, finished their homework and ran out to the tree house. Blaze, the family dog, followed them outside and wanted to play like he usually did after school.

"Not today, Blaze," said Cheryl. "We have business to do." They climbed up the old ladder to the tree house as fast as they could. They enjoyed the tree house that their dad had made for them. They had spent hours up in the house, and it had become a special place to think and plan. They could be alone with their private thoughts. When they climbed up into the tree house, they looked at each other with a blank stare. Each one was waiting for the other to speak. How are we going to tell others what skills they must use to be a Super Student? What are they? How many are there? These were the questions that were going through their heads as they looked out of one of the windows of the tree house.

End of session #1

★ GRADES 2-3 LEADER'S GUIDE (CONT.)

Lesson 1 Questions

Ask these questions in your community circle at the end of session #1.

- What was Cheryl and Daniel's problem?
- What is their dog's name?
- What is a club?
- Why did they go to their tree house?
- What will be some of their problems in starting the club?

Teachers/ Leaders

At the end of the day send home the parent permission sheet for the Super Student Program. This is to inform the parents of the Super Student Program and secure them as partners in this program. It is called Super Student Club Membership (See the Black line Masters at the end of this section for Grades 2-3). Use the second through fifth grade letter that is prepared for you. It is recommended that you read it with your students at the end of the day before they take it home.

The Super Student Test, True or False

Depending on the reading level of your children you could have them read this short fifteen question true/false questionnaire or you can read it to them and have them answer the true/false questions. This short questionnaire will get them ready for the concepts that will be taught in the next lessons. It will also give you an idea of what they are thinking about as you explore the Super Student concepts. You can use this as a pre-test and then give it at the end of Lesson 10. (See the Black line Masters at the end of this section for Grades 2-3).

© Youthlight, Inc.

Meeting Talon

It was a beautiful afternoon, and the trees were gently swaying in the breeze. All of a sudden, Cheryl noticed a large bird flying overhead. He seemed to be coming closer and closer to the tree house. He was beautiful and very large.

Suddenly a big noise of broken branches and a whoosh came through the open tree house window. Both children ducked down and fell to their faces as broken branches and leaves filled the tree house. When they picked themselves up a huge eagle lay limp on the other side of the tree house. The children crawled over to see the most beautiful bird they had ever seen. It had long brown wings with a large white head and a powerful beak.

"Oops, sorry, so sorry!" the bird said. Both kids jumped back shaking with fear.

"He talks!" said Cheryl.

"Oh yes, of course I talk." said the bird.

"Birds don't talk! Who are you? What do you want?" said Daniel.

"That's two questions. One at a time, please! My name is Talon. What do I want? I came to help you. You kids are hard to find. I judged my landing a little poorly, but I have had worse. I'm fine, just fine," the bird said as he brushed off the leaves and small branches from his feathers.

"You came to help us? Help us with what?" asked Cheryl.

"Didn't you want to start a Super Student Club?" asked the bird.

Both kids looked at each other in surprise and shock.

Meeting Talon (cont.)

"Yes," said Daniel, "but how did you know?"

"Oh, I have my ways," said Talon. "Long ago I had a dear friend teach me how to be a winner. My promise to him was to teach others the same skills that he taught me. So I have spent my whole life doing just that! It's my tribute to him. Where do you want to begin?"

The children still could not believe what they were seeing and hearing. Were they dreaming? In some ways, it felt like a dream. Time seemed to be standing still as they talked with this beautiful American bald eagle.

"Well, we want to start this club for all students at our school. We want to teach other kids how to do well in school so they will be happy in school and life. But, we don't know where to begin!" said Daniel. "What does it take to be a winner in school?"

Talon looked thoughtfully at the children as they were talking and then said, "They need to know the Super 8!"

"Super 8," said Cheryl looking at Daniel with a puzzling glance. "What is the Super 8?"

"Why the Super 8 are the eight skills that, if students focus on them, will bring them great rewards and happiness in school. These are the skills or the things that all good students do to be winners in school. They are the secrets that the best students use to be successful. The Super 8 are magic if they are used by students in class everyday. They will make students happy and successful!" With that Talon pulled out a map that had the words **SURVIVAL TREASURE KIT** on the top of the map. Two people named Keith and Christina had signed it!

Meeting Talon (cont.)

"Keith and Christina?" said Cheryl. "We have relatives named Keith and Christina!"

"Well, this is the map that they gave me for safe keeping and now it's yours." Talon said.

"Gave you?" said Daniel.

"Oh, it's a long story! Do you recognize the landmarks?" said Talon.

The children looked carefully at the map and noticed that the treasure map started behind the tree house near a stream.

"Yes, that's our stream behind the tree house!" Cheryl said. "Let's go!"

The children grabbed the map and climbed down the stairs of the tree house and ran to the stream that was just below the hill. Talon was already sitting on a huge rock near the stream when they arrived.

"You beat us!" said Daniel.

"Well, I have an advantage. I have wings!" said Talon. "Let's look at the map and see if we can find the treasure that will solve your problems."

The map did not seem hard to follow. First, they took 20 steps toward the east and found the large live oak tree. Then, they stepped 30 steps to the south and located the old pile of bricks. Finally they took 5 steps to the west and started to dig. The dirt was soft and easy to move. Soon they hit a chest with a picture of an eagle on the latch. As they brushed the dirt away they noticed how beautiful the chest was. It was almost brand new!

Meeting Talon (cont.)

"Open it," said Talon.

Daniel reached over, grabbed the latch and opened the lid. In the chest the children saw eight large eggs. Each one was a different color and they were glowing.

"You see," said Talon, "these are magic eggs with the power of changing students' behavior. Inside the eggs are the skills that will make Super Students. But the magic does not work unless the students want to be a Super Students! The students must want to win in school and be the best they can be. If they don't, the secrets and the magic will have no effect. Do your students want to be happy in school? Do they want to be Super Students?"

End of session # 2

GRADES 2-3 LEADER'S GUIDE (CONT.)

Lesson 2 Questions

Ask your students these questions. Have a good discussion.

- Describe the children's feelings when they first met Talon.
- What do you think the words SURVIVAL TREASURE KIT means on the top of the map?
- Why do you think Talon told the children that a student needs to want to be a Super Student to receive the magic of the skills?
- Who would like to learn the skills that are locked up in the magic eggs?
- Who would like to be a Super Student in our class?
- Who would like to be in the club? Why?

Would you like to try to draw the map?

I will reread the directions in this section after you have your paper and pencils ready (just use a clean sheet of paper). Have the children draw a compass with north, south, east, and west in the appropriate places in the top left hand corner of the paper. Start them in the center of the clean sheet of paper. Let them use dots to represent the steps. Have them draw in all the details including the chest.

REREAD THIS:

"The map did not seem hard to follow. First, they took 20 steps toward the east and found the large live oak tree. Then, they stepped 30 steps to the south and located the old pile of bricks. Finally they took 5 steps to the west and started to dig. The dirt was soft and easy to move. Soon they hit a chest with a picture of an eagle on the latch. As they brushed the dirt away they noticed how beautiful the chest was. It was almost brand new!"

Super Student Crossword Puzzle for Talon and the Magic Eggs.

This activity is a lot of fun for your students. Don't miss it! (See the Black line Masters at the end of this section for Grades 2-3).

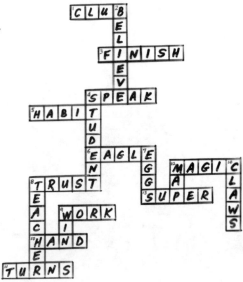

The White Egg

The children and Talon returned to the tree house with the chest and the magic eggs. "Let's open the first egg!" Cheryl said. "This is just what we need for the club."

"I'm ready to find out what the first skill is. I'll bet it is the most important one," said Daniel.

Talon took out the first egg. It was white. He cracked it with his strong beak. From inside the egg, a piece of paper fell out. It was as dry as could be. Daniel picked it up. The paper had the words in gold letters, **"I WILL LISTEN, OBEY, AND TRUST MY TEACHER."**

"This is first skill and the most important of all the skills. Your teacher cares for you and wants you to be happy and healthy. She/he wants you to learn all the important things in this grade

LESSON 3

The White Egg (cont.)

level so you can be a success. A Super Student listens to every word his/her teacher says and obeys the teacher every time she/he asks you to do something." said Talon.

"Even if you don't want to listen?" asked Cheryl.

"Yes, Cheryl. All of us feel from time to time that we do not want to listen or obey our teachers or parents. That's normal! But Super Students listen, anyway, even when they don't want to. Super Students force themselves to do what their teacher or parents want because they know it is for their own benefit. A funny thing happens when we listen even when we don't want to. We take control of our bad feelings, and it makes us happy!"

Both Daniel and Cheryl nodded their heads. They knew in their hearts that Talon was telling the truth. Daniel remembered one time he did not want to finish some work that the teacher had given him. He was just feeling lazy and wanted to work on a drawing he had started. He had had to push the bad feelings down and push himself to do the work. The work seemed boring at the time. When you are selfish and do your own thing after your teacher tells you differently, you know in your heart that you are wrong. Trusting your teacher to lead you in school is what being a student is all about.

"You have to be the boss over your mind and your body!" said Talon. "You're in control of your attitude!"

They could see why this was the most important skill. Can you?

End of session #3

GRADES 2-3 LEADER'S GUIDE (CONT.)

Lesson 3 Questions

Questions for discussion:

- What is the first skill to be a Super Student?
- Why is it important?
- Why is it hard to do this first skill sometimes?
- What did Talon mean that all students sometimes feel like they do not want to obey?
- What did Talon mean when he said, "You must be the boss over your body and your mind!"
- What did Talon mean when he said, "You're in control of your attitude!"
- What does attitude mean?

Teacher/ Leader

You can, at this time, tell your students what listening and obeying you means. Tell them what you are trying to accomplish by having them obey and trust you.

Essential Student Activity

Super Student Skill Worksheets

The Skill Sheets are designed to reinforce the lessons. Using them will develop your class into Super Students much faster. (See the Black line Masters at the end of this section for Grades 2-3).

Super Student Skill Worksheet #1
I WILL LISTEN, OBEY, AND TRUST MY TEACHER

Have your students work on this later in the day or use it during the next day before you start the next session. After the worksheet is finished and shared, you can send these worksheets home to be signed if you would like. When they return, you can save these worksheets (there are eight of them) in a personal Super Student folder. These worksheets and any of the activities can go home with the Super Student membership card, Focus Skills, pledge and certificate.

The Super Student Formula

You can let the children read this first and then go over it with them. They could cut each section out and paste it on a piece of construction paper. See if they can memorize what the letters stand for. They could cut out large letters S, U, P, E, and R. Have selected students read what the letters stand for during a group or grade level get together. This would be fun to do at a PTA meeting when you or your grade level chair is presenting the Super Student Program to the community. Have fun! (See the Black line Masters at the end of this section for Grades 2-3).

© Youthlight, Inc.

The Yellow Egg

Talon grabbed the second egg. It was colored yellow. He broke the egg again using his strong beak. Cheryl pulled the second skill out to read. In yellow writing it said, **"I WILL RAISE MY HAND TO SPEAK."**

"Wow," said Cheryl, "Now, we are getting down to what Super Students do to show they are super!"

"Yes," said Talon. "And this skill, like all the others, is very important. In school, boys and girls are in a room with lots of other students. If everyone is talking at the same time, no one can hear. Also, it is just good manners to speak one at a time. Good students know this, and they control themselves when they are in a group discussion."

"Even if another student calls out all the time?" asked Cheryl.

"Especially when that happens!" Talon said.

The Yellow Egg (cont.)

"I have a kid in my class who is always interrupting by calling out or talking to others students when the teacher is talking." replied Daniel.

"Is he a Super Student?" asked Talon.

"No, he always stays in for recess, and his mom is always coming in to talk with the teacher," said Daniel.

"That's my point," replied Talon. "Now, do you really think that he/she is a happy person?"

Both Daniel and Cheryl shook their heads no.

"The teacher controls the discussion in class. That's his/her job. We look to him/her to lead. We raise our hands to be noticed so we can be selected by the teacher to speak, even if other students who don't want to be Super Students keep yelling out. Super Students know this and use this skill every day in class. They know that taking turns and having manners is very important."

"One rule seems to build on the next one." Daniel said. "I need to listen, obey, and trust my teacher. Then, using the next rule helps me to show that I am a good listener when I raise my hand in class."

"That's good," said Talon.

"Do you raise your hand in class when you want to speak?"

End of session #4

GRADES 2-3 LEADER'S GUIDE (CONT.)

Lesson 4 Questions

Make sure your students are raising their hands to answer these questions. You could say, "I will call upon Super Students who raise their hands." Or, "I need you to raise your hand to answer these questions."

- What do you think of the story so far?
- Why should we raise our hand to answer and ask questions in class?
- What did Talon mean when he said, "It is good manners to raise your hand in class?"
- Why is asking questions just as good as answering questions?
- Who controls the discussion in class? Why?

Teachers/ Leaders

Super Student Skill Sheet #2
I WILL RAISE MY HAND TO SPEAK

Have your students work on this later in the day or use it during the next day before you start the next session. After the worksheet is finished and shared, send these worksheets home to be signed. When they return, you can save these worksheets (there are eight of them) in a personal Super Student folder. At the end of the story this folder will go home with the Super Student membership card and certificate.

SSS Super Student Stories

This is designed to warm your students up as they continue their growth. They will be looking for times when they were and were not acting like Super Students. Let them fill out the descriptions and then let them share if they would like to share. Don't force any student to share. (See the Black line Masters at the end of this section for Grades 2-3).

Raise your Hand Charts

This activity is a simple way to encourage students to raise their hands in class. You may only want to do this for a class or two because the children will start focusing on just raising their hands but it is effective to count up the number of times they participate. (See the Black line Masters at the end of this section for Grades 2-3).

**LESSON 5**

The Orange Egg

The third egg was orange. Talon managed to crack this egg open with a slight tap of his strong claws. The egg fell apart showing still another note. The paper was as dry as could be. The writing on the paper was in orange in large letters, **"I WILL THINK ALONG WITH THE SPEAKER."**

"What does that mean?" asked Cheryl.

"Oh, I think I know," said Daniel. "When anyone is speaking in class you must listen, really listen, to what they are saying. You should turn your head toward them and really follow what they are trying to say."

"Yes, that's right!" said Cheryl. "You will be learning from others as well as the teacher! I know a lot of kids who don't do it."

"Well, they are losing and missing out in school!" said Talon. "Remember we are talking about winning in school. Do both of you think along with the speaker?"

"I guess I could do better," admitted Daniel.

"Me too," said Cheryl.

"And your good body language will be noticed by the teacher and other students." said Talon.

"Body Language?" asked Cheryl.

"Yes, body language! The way you sit and hold yourself, the way you look at the speaker, and show the speaker that you are listening is called body language. It is very important in group behavior," added Talon.

The Orange Egg (cont.)

"I guess it has to do with manners again," said Daniel.

"That's right!" said Talon. "Manners have a lot to do with being a Super Student. The teacher notices all of this in class. He/she knows if you have manners and are trying to improve yourself. You can't fool him/her. In fact, you can't fool the students in your class. They know all about you. And they can see if you are trying to be a Super Student or not."

"Being a Super Student can be cool," said Daniel.

"Cool and also smart," replied Talon.

"Why would anyone want to lose at school?" asked Daniel.

"Good question!" said Talon.
 [Can you help Daniel with this question? Start some discussion].

I WILL THINK ALONG WITH THE SPEAKER

The Orange Egg (cont.)

"Kids, along with thinking with the speaker, I need to say something about asking good questions as Daniel just did." Daniel smiled. "You see, I know that Daniel is a Super Student and that he was listening to me because he asked a question about what I was talking about. Asking good questions is very important for Super Students. It allows them to stretch their minds. They grow smarter! But they have to be following the speaker's thoughts and asking good questions. In fact, it is better to ask questions than to have all the answers."

"One more thing," said Talon. "Even if the teacher does not pick you to answer a question, she still sees your hand. You don't have to be picked for every question for the teacher to see that you are trying to participate. Teachers want you to follow the lessons and the discussion. So, think along with the speaker by raising your hand to ask or answer questions, use good body language and manners in a group. All Super Students know these secrets."

"Sounds like a lot to learn!" said Cheryl.

"Not really," said Talon. "After a while, it becomes a good habit. Then, you won't even need to think about it, but you will need to practice every day! Can you ride a bike, Cheryl?"

© Youthlight, Inc.

The Orange Egg (cont.)

"Yes, of course!" said Cheryl. "Do you think about your feet and hands when you ride?"

"No, of course not. I just ride!" replied Cheryl. "Exactly!" said Talon. "It has become a habit."

The children looked at each other in amazement. This eagle was not a regular eagle, to say the least! He was smart! Super Smart! Both children felt so lucky to be having this happen to them. But they both felt as if they were still dreaming. Time seemed to have stopped! They were learning valuable lessons from an eagle. Would anyone believe them if they told what was happening?

End of session #5

GRADES 2-3 LEADER'S GUIDE (CONT.)

Lesson 5 Questions

- What does 'think along with the speaker' mean?
- Why is it important to 'think along with the speaker?'
- What is body language?
- Why is body language important in a group discussion?
- Why did Talon consider Daniel a Super Student?
- What did Talon mean when he said, "This will become a good habit after awhile."
- Why is asking good questions just as important as answering them?

Teachers/ Leaders

Super Student Skill Sheet #3
I WILL THINK ALONG WITH THE SPEAKER

Have your students work on this later in the day or use it during the next day before you start the next session. After the worksheet is finished and shared, send these worksheets home to be signed. When they return, you can save these worksheets (there are eight of them) in a personal Super Student folder that at the end of the story will go home with the Super Student membership card and certificate. (See the Black line Masters at the end of this section for Grades 2-3).

Super Student Week in Review

This is a short fifteen-question inventory that challenges your students to look at themselves in a critical way. It allows them to take at serious look at their personal behavior as a student. You can use this over and over during the year. Keeping copies of this in their personal portfolio allows them to see their growth. You can also use it at parent conferences. (See the Black line Masters at the end of this section for Grades 2-3).

© Youthlight, Inc.

LESSON 6

The Green Egg

The fourth egg was green. Although it looked hard, it cracked very easily when Talon pecked at it. Cheryl grabbed the note out of the eggshell pieces and said, **"I WILL BE PREPARED FOR MY WORK."** It was written in green ink.

"Why is this important?" said Cheryl.

"Being prepared with your books, papers, pencils, and notepads not only helps you to be ready to learn, but it also tells the teacher that you are serious about your job," said Talon.

"Job?" Cheryl asked.

"Yes, job," said Talon. Learning is a student's job. Your relatives have jobs that they go to every day.

"Yes, but they are paid for their jobs," Daniel explained.

"Well, students are paid for their work. It's called a report card!" Talon said.

The Green Egg (cont.)

"But that's not money," said Daniel.

"No, it's not… yet. It will be later in life, when you change reading and writing, doing math, science, and social studies into a job that pays real money," said Talon. "A lot of kids do not understand that what they are learning in school will be useful in their future jobs and careers. If you don't know very much or you can't do very much, you aren't paid very much! People are not going to pay you for jobs that you can't do. If you can't read, write, or do math, why would anyone pay you to do a job that requires you to use these skills. So, being prepared for your work in school becomes a Super Student skill. It is very important because it gets you ready to work on your future job."

End of Session #6

GRADES 2-3 LEADER'S GUIDE (CONT.)

Lesson 6 Questions

- What are some of the materials you need to have to be prepared for your work in school? Why?
- How is school like a job?
- What do employers think of workers who are not prepared for their work for that day?
- In what kinds of jobs is preparation for the work very important?

Teachers/ Leaders

Super Student Skill Sheet # 4
I WILL BE PREPARED FOR MY WORK

Have your students work on this later in the day or use it during the next day before you start the next session. After the worksheet is finished and shared, send these worksheets home to be signed. When they return, you can save these worksheets (there are eight of them) in a personal Super Student folder that at the end of the story will go home with the Super Student membership card, and certificate. (See the Black line Masters at the end of this section for Grades 2-3).

Super Student Focus Skills Checklist (Grades 2-5)

This activity starts your students looking critically at all the Focus Skills. These skills will become the guiding light for the standards that you are introducing to make them Super Students. They will be starting to judge themselves as life-long learners, in charge of becoming a Super Student themselves. After all, it is their job! Using this checklist on a daily basis is not too much. Many teachers pass it out every day and keep it on student's desks so students can fill it out near the end of the day. You can keep this in their portfolios or send it home on a daily or weekly basis.

Good For You! Caught You Being Good.

This is a sheet you will need as you catch students using the Super Student Focus Skills. It is vital that you use it! By catching students being good you are reinforcing correct behavior that makes Super Students. Use this often as you work with your students. Let them know that you notice and appreciate excellent work. Your students will give you more of the 'good stuff' if they know that you value their good behavior!

GRADES 2-3 LEADER'S GUIDE (CONT.)

Super Student To Do List

Students can use this list to keep themselves a little more organized. Let them fill it out at the beginning of the day. They can keep it on their desks and cross off the tasks as they are finished or write done after the task. (See the Black line Masters at the end of this section for Grades 2-3).

© Youthlight, Inc.

The Brown Egg

The fifth egg was brown. This egg seemed harder than any of the others thus far. Talon had to hit it three times with his strong beak to break the shell. When it finally broke the note flew up into the air. Daniel reached out and caught it.

"I have it!" said Daniel laughing.

"And I have you!" said Talon. "I caught you being good!"

"Caught me being good?" Daniel said curiously.

"Yes." said Talon. "You saved it from blowing away! Please read the fifth skill, Daniel."

Daniel read,
"I WILL GIVE MY BEST."

LESSON 7

The Brown Egg (cont.)

"Do you know why it is important?" said Talon.

"I guess so you receive hundreds on your papers," mentioned Cheryl.

"Not really," said Talon. "Super Students push themselves. They don't always receive hundreds on their papers or tests. They keep trying and trying. They don't quit. This life skill is called perseverance. They do their best! They know their teachers and relatives believe in them and, therefore, they believe in themselves. They push themselves to give their best in every job the teacher gives them. Their effort always pays off! They know that the harder you try, the more successful you are. When they start to feel lazy, they push themselves forward."

"Sounds like work," said Cheryl.

"Of course it is!" replied Talon. "But you receive nothing worthwhile in this life without working for it! I thought you knew that, Cheryl!"

"I guess, I did," said Cheryl.

Cheryl knew that you earn your way through school and life. She knew that you earn those grades on your report card and the Gold, Silver, and Bronze awards in the Celebration Program by working hard everyday. I guess you earn the right to be called a Super Student, she thought. If you don't work hard in school, you won't learn! No wonder you feel happy when you are a Super Student! You've earned it!

End of session #6

GRADES 2-3 LEADER'S GUIDE (CONT.)

Lesson 7 Questions

- How does school prepare you for your career or job in the future?
- What does 'giving your best' mean?
- Why is 'giving your best' important?
- What does 'caught being good' mean?
- Why do Super Students push themselves?
- What does it mean when someone says, "The harder you try the more successful you are!"
- Why is it important that you earn things in life?
- What did Cheryl learn about earning things in school?
- How does it feel when you work hard to earn something? Why?

Teachers/ Leaders

Super Student Skill Sheet #5
I WILL GIVE MY BEST

Have your students work on this later in the day or use it during the next day before you start the next session. After the worksheet is finished and shared, send these worksheets home to be signed. When they return, you can save these worksheets (there are eight of them) in a personal Super Student folder that at the end of the story will go home with the Super Student membership card and certificate. (See the Black line Masters at the end of this section for Grades 2-3).

© Youthlight, Inc.

The Red Egg

The sixth egg was red. Daniel noticed that it had some writing on the outside of the shell. This was the first egg to have any writing on the outside of the egg, and he was curious. He looked closer and asked if he could pick it up before Talon broke it open.

"Sure," said Talon, "Can you read the writing?"

It says, 'Beat the work. Don't let the work beat you'!"

"What in the world does that mean?" asked Cheryl.

"Let's find out!" said Talon. With one solid blow the red egg blew apart shooting the note onto the clubhouse floor. The kids looked carefully at the note. It said, **"I WILL FINISH ALL MY WORK."**

"This is the sixth Super Student skill," said Talon.

"Do you mean homework?" asked Cheryl.

"I mean all the work that the teacher gives you. Class work, homework, papers, projects, and assignments are all included. Everything the teacher gives you. You beat the work. Don't let the work beat you!"

"Why do you say it like that?" asked Cheryl.

"Because when you don't finish the work that your teacher has given you, the work has beaten you. You lose!"

"Do you mean like a game?" replied Daniel.

"If it is like a game, school is the most important game you will ever play. If you lose at it, it will hurt a lot. I don't want any boy or girl to hurt!" replied Talon.

The Red Egg (cont.)

The kids noticed that Talon had a tear rolling down his beautiful face. It rolled onto his beak. He wiped it away and continued.

"If you do not understand the work and it's hard to finish, go to your teacher for help. He/she needs to know. Don't keep it inside of you. Ask for help!"

"Start raising your hand!" said Cheryl trying to help Talon out.

"That's right!" said Talon. "Super Students seek help when they need it. They are not afraid to admit that they don't know it all! They look for people to help them if they are having a problem."

"Just like seeing your school counselor," said Daniel.

"That's correct!" said Talon. "Help is all around you. Teachers, counselors, and principals all want to help students. That's why they work in schools. They love to help children, and they want them to be happy and to learn. They don't stay up late at night thinking of ways to be nasty to students. They know how much you can handle in school. They know how much to give you so you learn all that you need to learn. Trust your teacher! Ask for help, then finish all the work and give your best every time."

Beat the work.

Don't let the work beat you!

"All these skills seem to work together!" said Cheryl.

"Now you're getting it!" said Talon smiling. "I'm proud of you!"

End of session #7

GRADES 2-3 LEADER'S GUIDE (CONT.)

Lesson 8 Questions

- What does 'beat the work' mean?
- What should you do if you are having problems with the work?
- Who can help you in school with problems?
- What does it say about your character or the way you are as a person if you don't give up on homework?
- Why do you think that someone who finishes his/her work all the time would be a good person to hire for a job?
- What is it saying about you if you have problems finishing your schoolwork and don't ask for help?
- What did Talon mean when he said, "School is the most important game you will ever play!"
- What did Cheryl mean when she said, "All these skills work together!"

Teachers/ Leaders

Super Student Skill Sheet #6
I WILL FINISH ALL MY WORK

Have your students work on this later in the day or use it during the next day before you start the next session. After the worksheet is finished and shared, send these worksheets home to be signed. When they return, you can save these worksheets (there are eight of them) in a personal Super Student folder that at the end of the story will go home with the Super Student membership card and certificate. (See the Black line Masters at the end of this section for Grades 2-3).

Beating the Work

There is something about finishing your work that makes you feel good! This activity allows students to color the magic eggs when they finish the assignments for the day. (See the Black line Masters at the end of this section for Grades 2-3).

The Blue Egg

The seventh egg was blue. It seemed to be changing shades from light blue to dark blue and then starting all over again.

"Why is it changing color, Talon?" said Cheryl.

"It is trying to get our attention. It is telling us about feeling blue or sad." replied Talon.

"And you will be sad if you don't do the seventh skill of a Super Student! All the other skills have to do with your work with the teacher. But school is also about working with others. There are lots of boys and girls in school. Just look around! Some students have told me, 'I could be a great student if there were no other students in my class.' What they are saying is that other students are stopping or distracting them from being a great student. You must overcome this. That's why this skill is so important! Let's have a look!" Talon said.

Talon took a big jump into the air and came down on the egg crushing it all to pieces. Cheryl picked out the note. It was written in blue ink. Cheryl noticed that even the ink was also turning different shades of the color blue. This must be important she thought! The note read, **"I WILL WORK OUT PROBLEMS WITH OTHERS."**

"I knew that we were going to talk about this one!" said Daniel.

"What does it mean?" asked Cheryl.

"It means that a Super Student knows that schools don't permit fighting, hitting, yelling, and screaming," said Talon.

"Some students will try to lead you into trouble by getting you so mad that you lose your cool and start a fight or you say bad words.

LESSON 9

The Blue Egg (cont.)

"They know how to push your buttons so that you lose your temper!" said Daniel.

"What should we do?" asked Daniel.

"I'm glad you're interested, Daniel. This problem can ruin you, even if you are a pretty good student in the first place. If you want to stay a Super Student you must stay out of trouble, and you can! Here are the secrets."

The children leaned toward Talon. They knew this was a big problem in school because many times students would tease or try to lead you into trouble. They wondered what to do because they often felt like fighting back.

Talon spoke, "When you feel angry, you need to know how to calm down and remove yourself from the problem. Remember where you are! Talk it out and work it out, first. Do it calmly. If that doesn't work, move away from the problem. Take three deep breaths or count backwards slowly. Think nice thoughts, and then,

The Blue Egg (cont.)

look for an adult to tell. You can talk to a teacher, counselor, or principal. But the most important thing is that you try to work it out before you find yourself in a word fight or a fistfight! Don't hit it out, kick it out or swear it out. If you do, you have gone too far, and you are acting just as badly as the kid who is bothering you."

"The other kids might call us a sissy if we don't fight," said Cheryl.

"They might," said Talon. "But they won't be going to the principal's office with you when you meet with your parents and the principal! They will be back in the classroom laughing. It takes a smarter, better person to try to work it out and walk away. Super Students know that they can't afford to wind up in the principal's office because of a fight or problems with others."

"So they talk it out, work it out, or move it out!" said Daniel.

"I like that! Sounds good!" said Talon. "You are the only one who suffers when you blow up. You can't worry about the other kids. Listen, your relatives, your teacher, counselor, and principal are some of the people who really care about you."

"What about your friends?" Cheryl asked.

"If they are real friends, they will want you safe and out of trouble. If they want you in trouble, they're not your friends!"

Cheryl and Daniel smiled. They knew Talon was telling the truth. Now they had something they could do when those bullies tried to lead them into trouble. They understood now that others don't lead you into trouble. You lead yourself into trouble. You are the boss over your body and your mind, thought Daniel. And he was right!

End of session #8

GRADES 2-3 LEADER'S GUIDE (CONT.)

Lesson 9 Questions

- Why can this problem ruin Super Students?
- What were some of the secrets that Talon shared with the kids concerning this problem?
- What did Talon mean when he said, "Your teacher, counselor, and principal are some of the people that really care for you?"
- What would true friends do if you were being bullied or teased? How could they help?
- What did Daniel mean when he said, "You are the boss over your body and mind?"
- What should you do if someone is teasing, bullying or bothering you?

Teachers/ Leaders

Super Student Skill Sheet #7
I WILL WORK OUT PROBLEMS WITH OTHERS

Have your students work on this later in the day or use it during the next day before you start the next session. After the worksheet is finished and shared, send these worksheets home to be signed. When they return, you can save these worksheets (there are eight of them) in a personal Super Student folder that at the end of the story will go home with the Super Student membership card and certificate. (See the Black line Masters at the end of this section for Grades 2-3).

© Youthlight, Inc.

The Black Egg

The eighth and last egg was black. Black is such a strong color. I guess that is why it is used as the color for the last belt level in karate. It means the best, excellent, or master.

Cheryl and Daniel looked at the last black egg in the carton. They had gone through white, yellow, orange, green, brown, red, and blue magic eggs and had learned a lot from the Super Student Skills. What could this last egg hold? What skill could this last egg reveal that they had not heard already? Cheryl thought that they already had the most important skills necessary to start the club.

The children quickly thought about their adventures with Talon that would be a great help in starting their Super Student Club to help other students. They wanted so much to be able to share what a winner in school does. Now they had seven skills on which they could focus. Talon's voice broke the silence.

"Kids, you have learned some important things to help you start your club."

"Yes, we have," said Cheryl. "You have been an answer to our prayers. We can now start our club and share the skills with our whole school!"
"Good, that's why I came. With this egg, we have come full circle. This last egg is very special to me." Talon paused for a moment and then said, "This last skill is like the first skill. It is very important."

"What is it, Talon?" said Daniel.

"Let's see. You open it!" said Talon.

"How?" Cheryl said.

"Close your eyes and think about something beautiful and good."

The Black Egg (cont.)

The children looked at each other and shrugged their shoulders.

"Come on kids. You can do it!" said Talon.

Cheryl and Daniel closed their eyes and smiled. They heard a popping sound and quickly opened their eyes to see the black egg explode in front of them. A note in large black letters remained.

"Wow!" said Cheryl.

"Mind blowing!" said Daniel as he picked up the note and read, **"I WILL HAVE A POSITIVE, HEALTHY ATTITUDE."**

"What is that?" asked Cheryl. It must be important because Talon is very serious about this skill, thought Cheryl.
[Please pause for a little discussion to see if any students can discuss this. Why is this important?]

"A positive, healthy attitude really identifies a Super Student!" declared Talon. "Attitude is the way you feel about things. Besides the way you act and behave, it is one of the few things in life that you have control over. You did not choose your family or where and when you were born. You did not choose the school you are going to or the teacher you have. But, you can choose to be happy or sad, helpful or hurtful. Remember you are in control of your body and mind! You decide what you say and do in every situation."

"Is that why you said that we can decide what to do when someone bothers us in school?" asked Daniel.

"That's right! You decide how to act in those situations." Talon replied.

"Sometimes we make mistakes," remarked Cheryl.

© Youthlight, Inc.

LESSON 10: The Black Egg (cont.)

"Of course, we all make mistakes!" said Talon.

"But only a fool continues to make the same mistake over and over. If you decide to be a winner in school, you will practice and pick up the Super Student skills that show others that you are winning in school. Your attitude reflects if you are a hard worker or a quitter in school. It shows if you have manners and respect or if you are selfish and spoiled. Your attitude is controlled only by you."

"I had a friend who was sick in the hospital, and he was still happy and excited to talk to me. He taught me that I have a lot to be thankful for. I guess it was his attitude that taught me that!" Cheryl remarked.

"Good story, Cheryl. That friend's attitude is what was shinning through. He was happy even though he was in a bad situation."

The Black Egg (cont.)

Talon said. "That's why you remember your friend. You can't blame anyone else for your attitude. You can take full credit for it. So, you can control your attitude about school. Bad as well as good things happen to everyone, but how you react to them is what makes the difference! You can control how you act and behave. The Super Student Focus Skills will help you along the way. Most of all, you should be thankful for everything that you already have."

"Do you mean we should count our blessings?" said Daniel.

"Exactly! Always look at the bright side. Put on a positive, healthy attitude and use the Super Students Focus Skills that you have discovered in the magic eggs today. Good things will happen to you! That's a promise!"

With that Talon gave the children a big smile.
"I have something for you and your Super Student club members," said Talon.

He reached in his back feathers and pulled out a rolled up piece of paper. Then he said, "Please read it Daniel."

Daniel unrolled the paper and began to read:

> "My attitude is the only thing I can control. I can choose to be happy or sad, helpful or hurtful. I can choose to be a winner in school. My attitude is shown in these Super Student skills. I will read these Focus skills everyday. I will practice these skills to show I am a winner. People will see me using these skills, and good things will happen to me. As I focus on these skills, I will feel good and happy inside. Being good is good for me! I really want to be a winner in school. And I know I can be!"

"This can be our club pledge!" said Daniel. "It would make me very

The Black Egg (cont.)

happy if you would use it," said Talon.

"Great!" Cheryl said. "Then we have all we need to start the club! We have the skills and the pledge!"

Talon smiled and the children could see he was very happy. "All you need now is the other students to join to be Super Students. They will need to be able to follow the rules," said Talon.

"Oh, we'll find the students! Everyone will want to sign up!" said Daniel.

"My job is done then. I need both of you to close your eyes."

The children looked at each other. Were they going to lose a dear friend?

"We'll miss you, Talon!" said Daniel.

"I'll be here if you need me. Just look out of the window of the tree house and say the pledge. I'm that close!"

With that Daniel and Cheryl closed their eyes. They heard a loud noise like a bang and quickly opened their eyes again. Talon was gone. At first, they were confused. Had they dreamed of this encounter with Talon? No, they could see the notes and the pledge still on the treehouse floor. It was real! They were ready to start the club.

"Do you think that the students in the other classes will join?" asked Cheryl. "I hope so," said Daniel. "Let's ask them!"

End of session # 9

GRADES 2-3 LEADER'S GUIDE (CONT.)

Teacher/ Leaders

Super Student Skill Sheet #8
I WILL HAVE A POSITIVE, HEALTHY ATTITUDE.

Have your students work on this later in the day. After the worksheet is finished and shared, send these worksheets home to be signed. When they return, you can save these worksheets (there are eight of them) in a personal Super Student folder that at the end of the story will go home with the Super Student membership card and certificate.
(See the Black line Masters at the end of this section for Grades 2-3).

★ After the Super Student Skill Sheet #8 is finished, ask your class:
"Who would like to sign up for our Super Student Club? Do you believe that you can be super? Can you follow the rules and promise to keep trying even if you have a problem once in a while?"

★ Distribute the Take the Pledge Commitment Sheet. Read it with the students (See the Black line Masters at the end of this section for Grades 2-3).

"This is our commitment sheet. I'm going to ask you to sign up if you are ready to join the Super Student Club. By signing this you are saying that you will practice the Super Student Focus Skills every day and abide by the Super Student Pledge."

★ Distribute the Super Student Membership Cards, Certificates, Focus Skills, and Pledge as a Packet to go home. (See the Black line Masters at the end of this section for Grades 2-3).

The Super Student Pledge Word Find

Have your students use the Pledge Word Find. This activity is simple but fun and a good tool for your students to learn the pledge. Have the students check the word find against their copy of the pledge. (See the Black line Masters at the end of this section for Grades 2-3).

The Super Student Focus Skills Checklist
(Highly recommended)

Have your students use this checklist at least twice a week to keep tabs on their attitude and behavior. This checklist is very useful for arrangements that you have with parents on daily reports that need to go home concerning their student's behavior. This checklist is an excellent form to monitor your Super Student Club members before the Awards Celebration. (See the Black line Masters at the end of this section for Grades 2-3).

© Youthlight, Inc.

GRADES 2-3 LEADER'S GUIDE (CONT.)

Teacher/Leaders

★ Send home the Super Student Focus Skills and Pledge Memorization. (See the Black line Masters at the end of this section for Grades 2-3). This prepared parent letter secures the parents as partners for the memorization of the Super Student Focus Skills and the Pledge.

★ Also, make sure you copy the Super Student Focus Sheet and My Pledge for the students to have at their desks or tape them on the wall to refer to (See the Black line Masters at the end of this section for Grades 2-3).

★ You will need to reinforce the Focus Skills and My Pledge each week in community circle by going over the Skills and having your children memorize the pledge. Keep them displayed in the room. With their parents' help, the students can memorize the Focus Skills and My Pledge. I highly recommend that they do. Point out during the week who has been doing which skill and how happy you are that your students are developing into Super Students.

★ It is very important to celebrate students and their school efforts and achievements. I recommend that you celebrate your students at report card period. They can be rewarded with medals, trophies, or certificates. Or better yet, celebrate them every interim period. Start today and make a big deal out of being a Super Student!

Counselors

This program allows you to involve a whole school in celebrating excellence and achievement grade by grade. Research has proven that effective schools focus on student effort and recognition of achievement (Marzano, 2001). As you spearhead the Super Student Program and direct the Celebration Awards program, you will be having a major impact on your school that is measurable and effective. This will fit into any goals-based guidance program for the elementary schools. If you have the use of a TV studio in your school, your follow up in class and by TV will be very supportive to your teachers.

★ THE *SUPER STUDENT* CLUB PACKET FOR GRADES 2-3

A tool is only good if you use it. The Super Student Program will only help you in the classroom if you use the concepts and skills. It is a tool, a survival kit, for you and your children. As you refer to the skills when you see them being used by your children, the students will respond and work harder for you. They will become the Super Students that you want. Be patient and persistent. After a while, these skills will become a habit and a way for your students to be successful in school. It will serve them not only with you this year but in future grades. In addition, it will become something that they will use as they progress into the world of work.

After the student signs the commitment sheet, his/her packet includes; the Super Student Focus Skills Sheet, the pledge, membership card and certificate. Many teachers place the Super Student Focus Skills Sheet and My Pledge right on the student's desk or on a bulletin board with each child's membership cards. Keeping the Super Student Focus Skills nearby allows you to visit the concepts during the day, if needed.

Teachers, many times, will take pictures with the students holding the membership cards. They will display the pictures where all visitors can see them. Teachers, send home the parent letters (see the Black line masters). In any case, it is important to display and continue to work with the concepts and skills during the community circle or group time throughout the year.

If you start the program at the beginning of the school year, I suggest that you have a mid-year contest for memorizing the Super Student Focus Skills and My Pledge. Enclosed in the Black line masters is a sample letter to the parents for this memorization challenge.

The more you celebrate your Super Students and draw attention to the Focus Skills and the Super Student Club the more your students will improve their Super Student behavior. I cannot stress this vital repetition to develop the skills so that they are habitual. Young children love this repetition.

The use of The Super Student Focus Skills Checklist (a Black line master) is highly recommended to get ready for the Awards Celebration. Have your students use this checklist at least twice a week to keep tabs on their attitude and behavior before the marking period is over. This checklist is very useful for arrangements that you have with parents on daily reports that need to go home concerning their student's behavior. This checklist is an excellent form to monitor your Super Student Club members before the Awards Celebration.

Please use any of the worksheet exercises in the Black line masters to bring your students the needed reminder of using the skills on a daily basis.

The parent information should go home. You will need to continue to secure the parent's cooperation for the program throughout the year. Remember to celebrate the winners of the club at each report card time. These are students who are using most of the skills on a regular basis. Look at the skills with them. Are they listening, raising their hand, being prepared for their work, giving their best, finishing their work, working out problems with others, and producing a positive healthy attitude in class? If so, they need to be celebrated.

Our school calls this a Renaissance Celebration, and we do it four times a year school-wide. I cannot stress using this celebration and recognition enough. It is vital that your school celebrates at least four times a year the product you are producing, namely, students.

If your school has not adopted the Super Student Program school-wide, you can do this celebration in your classroom after report cards are given out. Invite the parents of the winners to the celebration. Encourage picture taking and serve refreshments. Celebrate your students!

© Youthlight, Inc.

The SUPER STUDENT Program

Reproducible Blackline Masters for grades 2-3

© Youthlight, Inc.

★ SUPER STUDENT CLUB MEMBERSHIP

Dear Parents of Second through Fifth Grade Students,

We are beginning a special program, called the Super Student Club at our school. This program will reinforce our instruction and achievement on a daily basis.

We need your help!
The Super Student Club was developed to help students:
- Take responsibility for their learning.
- Learn a systemic model for improving their schoolwork.
- Improve their effort toward academic tasks.
- Absorb basic study skills and concepts that improve the effectiveness and efficiency of their learning.
- Enhance self-esteem.
- Develop lifelong learners with positive healthy attitudes.

How can you help?
Please go over the Focus Skills and My Pledge with your child. He/she will have to learn and do these skills every day. Please support your child's teacher and sign this permission slip so they can join the Super Student Club. We believe that any student can be a Super Student. It is all about a super attitude! Please call us at the school if you have any questions.

★ Super Student Focus Skills

1. I will listen, obey, and trust my teacher.
2. I will raise my hand to speak.
3. I will think along with the speaker.
4. I will be prepared for my work.
5. I will give my best.
6. I will finish all my work
7. I will work out problems with others.
8. I will have a positive, healthy attitude.

★ My Pledge

My attitude is the only thing I can control in life. I can choose to be happy or sad, helpful or hurtful. I can choose to be a winner in school. My attitude is reflected in these Super Student FOCUS Skills. I will read these Focus Skills every day. I will practice these skills to show I am a winner. People will see me doing these skills and good things will happen to me! As I focus on these skills, I will feel happy inside. Being GOOD is good for me! I really want to be a winner in school.

I give permission for my child to be in the Super Student Club. I will support the program. I will go over the Focus Skills and My Pledge with my child and keep in touch with his/her teacher throughout the year.

Child's name_____

Teacher_____ Grade_____

Parent Signature_____

© Youthlight, Inc.

The Super Student Test
TRUE OR FALSE

1. Anyone can be a Super Student if he/she wants to badly enough.   T   F

2. It is OK, if you talk when the teacher is teaching.   T   F

3. It is not important to raise your hand in class to ask or answer a question.   T   F

4. You don't have to listen to your teacher to be a good student.   T   F

5. Listening to other students in class when it is their turn to talk is not important.   T   F

6. Being prepared for your work in school is very important.   T   F

7. Your teacher can tell when you are not giving your best.   T   F

8. Giving your best in school is not very important.   T   F

9. You can be a good student and not finish your work.   T   F

10. Getting into fights and problems with others will not hurt you as a student.   T   F

11. School is not that important.   T   F

12. Having a positive attitude has nothing to do with success.   T   F

13. Super Students are born not made.   T   F

14. You can be a good student regardless of your family's economic situation.   T   F

15. You can be a Super Student regardless of your race or culture.   T   F

The Super Student Crossword Puzzle
TALON AND THE MAGIC EGGS

ACROSS

1. We will form a Super Student _____.
3. I must _____ all of my work.
4. I must raise my hand to _____.
5. A _____ is something that I do over and over without thinking about it.
6. Talon is this kind of bird.
8. I must _____ my teacher to help me to do my best.
9. I must finish all of my _____.
10. When I raise my _____ my teacher knows that I have something to say.
11. In class we must take _____ speaking.
12. The eggs in this story were _____ eggs.
13. This is the kind of student I want to be.

DOWN

2. You must _____ that you can be a winner in school.
4. I want to be a Super _____.
7. Birds lay _____.
8. My _____ in school is there to help me learn.
9. I want to _____ the game called school.
12. A _____ helps me to find my way.
14. Talon has these at the end of his feet.

The Super Student Skill Sheet
TALON & THE MAGIC EGGS

Skill #1
I WILL LISTEN, OBEY, AND TRUST MY TEACHER.

Super Student _____ Grade _____ Teacher _____

Write the first Super Student Focus Skill on this line.

_____

What does this mean to you?

_____

Describe a time today that you did not want to listen, obey, or trust your teacher.

_____

☺ Every time I listen, obey, and trust my teacher today, I will place a SMALL smiley face under the correct column.

LISTEN   **OBEY**   **TRUST**

Parents/Guardian signature_____
THINK LIKE A WINNER! ACT LIKE A WINNER! BE A WINNER!

THE SUPER FORMULA

S **stands for SELF.** You must decide for yourself to become a Super Student. No one can do this for you. You can do it for your parents, relatives, teachers, or friends, but the decision to become a good student is yours alone. Nobody can make you a great student. The magic lies within you.

U **stands for UNDERSTAND.** You must understand the consequences of not doing well in school. You are throwing away time and possibilities when you are not becoming all that you can be. You can't make up time. We are all given just twenty-four hours a day, seven days a week. Once this time is gone, you will not get more. If you are wasting your years in elementary school, how will you get them back?

P **stands for PERSONAL.** Deciding to become a Super Student is a personal decision. Your mom or dad can't make it for you. Your attitude is the only thing you can control in life. It is a personal decision you make about how you will conduct each day of your life. If you make a personal decision to follow the Super Student Focus Skills, good things will happen to you.

E **stands for EFFORT.** Your effort counts! The more you try to become a SUPER STUDENT the more you will succeed! When you are working hard, it becomes evident to you and all who are around you. ATTITUDE + EFFORT = RESULTS

R **stands for RESULTS.** You will become a SUPER student when you are focusing on the correct skills and the giving the required effort. You will then get the results that you want! Working hard, learning, achieving, acquiring good grades, and becoming happy about yourself as a student are goals you can achieve.

The Super Student Skill Sheet
TALON & THE MAGIC EGGS

Skill #2
I WILL RAISE MY HAND TO SPEAK.

Super Student _____ Grade _____ Teacher _____

Write the second Super Student Focus Skill on this line.

_____

✓ Put a check mark every time you raise your hand to answer or ask a question during one of your classes. Place check marks here:

Total number of checks_____

Congratulations! Can you make this into a good habit?

Why should we raise our hands in class?

_____

_____

What do manners have to do with raising your hand in class?

_____

_____

Parents/Guardian signature_____

THINK LIKE A WINNER! ACT LIKE A WINNER! BE A WINNER!

SSS
SUPER STUDENT STORIES

Use the spaces below to write about experiences from your student life.

Describe a time when you obeyed and trusted your teacher.

_____
_____
_____
_____
_____

Describe a time when you were not prepared for your work.

_____
_____
_____
_____
_____

Describe a time you did not give your best.

_____
_____
_____
_____

Describe a time when you worked out a problem with another student.

_____
_____
_____
_____

RAISE YOUR HAND CHARTS

Student Activity 2.6

Super Student _____   Date _____

Teacher _____   Grade _____

Write the name of the class and then use tally marks for each time you raise your hand to ask or answer a question. Count up the number of times that you raise your hand in a class period. You will be surprised how many times your hand is going up! Remember the teacher does not need to pick you every time. Just so she sees that you are listening and able to ask and answer questions.

CLASS	TALLY MARKS	TOTAL
1.		
2.		
3.		
4.		
5.		
6.		

TOTAL NUMBER OF TALLYS FOR ALL CLASSES _____

The Super Student Skill Sheet

Skill #3
I WILL THINK ALONG WITH THE SPEAKER.

Super Student _____ Grade _____ Teacher _____

Write the third Super Student Focus Skill on this line.

_____

✔ *Check it out in class!*

Do you think along with the speakers in your class?
Are you listening and thinking with teachers and students when they are talking?

Pick a Class _____

My eyes were on the speaker.	❑ yes	❑ no
My body language was great.	❑ yes	❑ no
I was an active listener.	❑ yes	❑ no
I answered a question during the class.	❑ yes	❑ no
I asked a question during the class.	❑ yes	❑ no
I did not talk when others were speaking.	❑ yes	❑ no
I can say the first three skills so far.	❑ yes	❑ no

Parents/Guardian signature_____

THINK LIKE A WINNER! ACT LIKE A WINNER! BE A WINNER!

© Youthlight, Inc.

SUPER STUDENT WEEK IN REVIEW

Student Activity 2.7

Today's date _____

Your Name _____

Think back on the week in this classroom. Read each statement, and then check the column that best describes how you feel about your behavior in school.

THIS WEEK IN SCHOOL	All of the time	Most of the time	Some of the time	Never
1. I respected my teacher.				
2. I obeyed my teacher.				
3. I trusted my teacher.				
4. I listened to my teacher.				
5. I raised my hand to answer questions.				
6. I was respectful to others.				
7. I treated others with respect.				
8. I helped others.				
9. I was prepared for my work.				
10. I gave my best in class.				
11. I finished my work.				
12. I worked out problems with others.				
13. I had a positive, healthy attitude.				
14. I felt accepted.				
15. I felt appreciated.				

Student Activity Essential

The Super Student Skill Sheet

TALON & THE MAGIC EGGS

Skill #4

I WILL BE PREPARED FOR MY WORK.

Super Student _____ Grade _____ Teacher _____

Write the fourth Super Student Focus Skill on this line.

_____

✓ **Put a check mark by these Super Student tools if you have the supplies or have done the task.**

- ❏ Pencils
- ❏ Paper
- ❏ Books
- ❏ Folders

- ❏ Homework ready for today
- ❏ My desk neat and clean
- ❏ Other supplies ready

How is school like a job?

Pick a relative or a friend who has a job.
Tell us how that person must be ready for that job every morning.

Parents/Guardian signature_____

THINK LIKE A WINNER! ACT LIKE A WINNER! BE A WINNER!

© Youthlight, Inc.

SUPER STUDENT FOCUS SKILLS CHECKLIST

Student Activity 2.8

Did you use these skills today?

Place a smiley face in front of each skill that you did all day long.

Today is _____

Super Student _____

Teacher _____ Grade _____

_____ I did listen, obey, and trust my teacher.

_____ I did raise my hand to speak.

_____ I did think along with the speaker.

_____ I was prepared for my work.

_____ I did give my best.

_____ I did finish all my work.

_____ I did work out problems with others.

_____ I did have a positive, healthy attitude.

How many smiley faces did you get today? _____

Teacher Comments:

Parent signature_____

132

© Youthlight, Inc.

GOOD FOR YOU!

Student Activity 2.9

YOU GOT CAUGHT BEING GOOD.

_____ **DID SOMETHING SPECIAL.** You used these Super Student Focus Skills in class. Thank you for being a Super Student.

Date _____

✓ **Here are the skills that you used.**
(check all that apply)

_____ I did listen, obey, and trust my teacher.

_____ I did raise my hand to speak.

_____ I did think along with the speaker.

_____ I was prepared for my work.

_____ I did give my best.

_____ I did finish all my work.

_____ I did work out problems with others.

_____ I did have a positive, healthy attitude.

© Youthlight, Inc.

SUPER STUDENT TO DO LIST

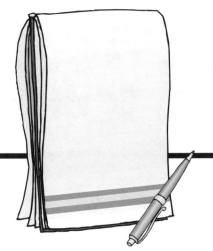

Things to do today:

✓ Make a list of what you need to do today! Be prepared for your work. Put a check in the box beside the task when you finish.

☐ 1. _____
☐ 2. _____
☐ 3. _____
☐ 4. _____
☐ 5. _____
☐ 6. _____
☐ 7. _____
☐ 8. _____
☐ 9. _____
☐ 10. _____
☐ 11. _____
☐ 12. _____
☐ 13. _____
☐ 14. _____
☐ 15. _____

DID YOU GET IT ALL DONE? ☐ Yes ☐ No

The Super Student Skill Sheet

TALON & THE MAGIC EGGS

Skill #5

I WILL GIVE MY BEST.

Super Student _____ Grade _____ Teacher _____

Write the fifth Super Student Focus Skill on this line.

_____

I GAVE MY BEST IN:

(Circle please)

Math   **Specials**   **Behavior in the hallway**
Reading   **Behavior on the bus/coming to school** **Behavior at recess**
Writing
Science   **Behavior at breakfast/lunch**   **Behavior with others**
Social Studies

Tell about how you gave your best in one of the above.

What does 'giving your best' mean?

Parents/Guardian signature_____

THINK LIKE A WINNER! ACT LIKE A WINNER! BE A WINNER!

The Super Student Skill Sheet
TALON & THE MAGIC EGGS

Skill #6

I WILL FINISH ALL MY WORK.

Super Student _____ Grade _____ Teacher _____

Write the sixth Super Student Focus Skill on this line.

_____

☺ Put a smiley face under the subject(s) that you finished all your work in today.

Math   **Reading**   **Spelling**   **Word Work**   **Science**   **Social Studies**

Did you beat the work today?   ☐ yes   ☐ no

How did it feel? _____

Draw a picture here showing you finishing your work in class.

Parents/Guardian signature_____

THINK LIKE A WINNER! ACT LIKE A WINNER! BE A WINNER!

Student Activity 2.11

BEATING THE WORK

**Finishing all your work is very important in school!
CONGRATULATIONS to you when you BEAT THE WORK!**

Super Student _____ Grade _____ Teacher _____

Color the magic eggs when you finish your work in these subject areas.

Total number of colored magic eggs: _____   *Great Work!*

Student Activity Essential

The Super Student Skill Sheet
TALON & THE MAGIC EGGS

Skill #7
I WILL WORK OUT PROBLEMS WITH OTHERS.

Super Student _____ Grade _____ Teacher _____

Write the seventh Super Student Focus Skill on this line.

_____

☺ Every time I work out a problem with others today, I will place a smiley face here and write a short note telling about what happened. I can talk it out, work it out, and move it out!

My Day:

What are some of the tricks you can use if someone continues to bother you? Remember the story suggestions!

Parents/Guardian signature_____

THINK LIKE A WINNER! ACT LIKE A WINNER! BE A WINNER!

© Youthlight, Inc.

The Super Student Skill Sheet
TALON & THE MAGIC EGGS

Skill #8

I WILL HAVE A POSITIVE, HEALTHY ATTITUDE.

Super Student _____ Grade _____ Teacher _____

Write the eighth Super Student Focus Skill on this line.

_____

I'm counting my blessings! Draw three pictures of the things you are thankful for. Beside the pictures, tell why you are thankful.

Picture #1

Picture #2

Picture #3

Parents/Guardian signature_____

THINK LIKE A WINNER! ACT LIKE A WINNER! BE A WINNER!

TAKE THE PLEDGE!

COMMITMENT SHEET

My Pledge

My attitude is the only thing I can control in life. I can choose to be happy or sad, helpful or hurtful. I can choose to be a winner in school. My attitude is reflected in these Super Student FOCUS Skills. I will read these Focus Skills every day. I will practice these skills to show I am a winner. People will see me doing these skills and good things will happen to me! As I focus on these skills, I will feel happy inside. Being GOOD is good for me! I really want to be a winner in school.

I am signing this commitment sheet with my classmates and accepting my membership card for the Super Student Club. By signing this commitment sheet, I am saying that I want to be a Super Student and will use the Super Student Focus Skills everyday. My teacher has the right and responsibility to correct me when I stray from the Focus Skills and Pledge. I will also say the Pledge and abide by this Super Student Code. My teacher believes that I can be a Super Student. If I believe that I can, it will happen with hard work!

Signed:_____ Date: _____

Teacher_____ Grade _____

© Youthlight, Inc.

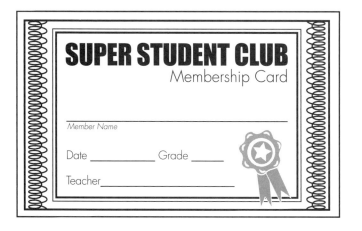
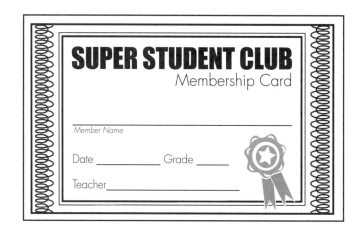
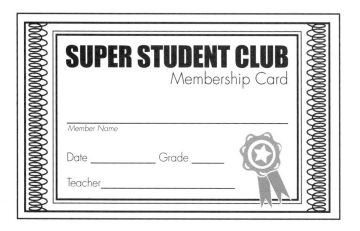
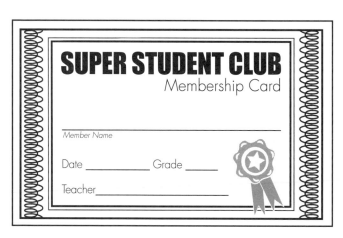
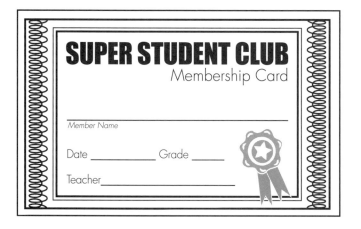
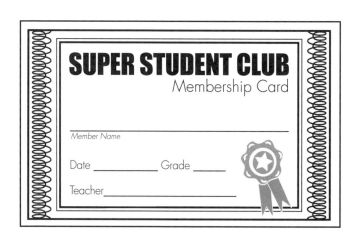

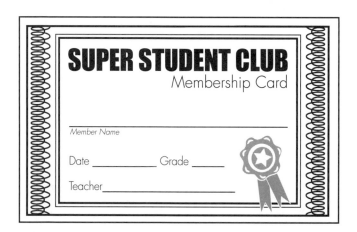

SUPER STUDENT
Certificate

This certifies that

_____

Has used the Focus Skills in class, has taken the Super Student Pledge, and is officially in the Super Student Club.

Teacher _____   Date _____

★ FOCUS SKILLS ★

1. I will listen, obey, and trust my teacher.
2. I will raise my hand to speak.
3. I will think along with the speaker.
4. I will be prepared for my work.
5. I will give my best.
6. I will finish all my work
7. I will work out problems with others.
8. I will have a positive, healthy attitude.

My Pledge

My attitude is the only thing I can control in life. I can choose to be happy or sad, helpful or hurtful. I can choose to be a winner in school. My attitude is reflected in these Super Student FOCUS Skills. I will read these Focus Skills every day. I will practice these skills to show I am a winner. People will see me doing these skills and good things will happen to me! As I focus on these skills, I will feel happy inside. Being GOOD is good for me! I really want to be a winner in school.

THE SUPER STUDENT PLEDGE

Find the eight missing words in the pledge.

My Pledge

My _____ is the only thing I can control in life. I can _____ to be happy or sad, helpful or hurtful. I can _____ to be a _____ in school. My attitude is reflected in these Super Student FOCUS _____. I will _____ these Focus Skills every day. I will practice these skills to show I am a winner. People will see me doing these skills and _____ things will happen to me! As I focus on these skills, I will feel happy inside. Being GOOD is good for me! I really want to be a _____ in school.

SUPER STUDENT FOCUS SKILLS & PLEDGE MEMORIZATION

Dear Parents of Second through Fifth Grade Students,

We need your help!
As you know, we have started the most important club your child can be part of at our school . . . The Super Student Club! This special program reinforces our instruction and achievement on a daily basis. The Super Student Club was developed so we could remind students daily about the skills that make winners in school. As you are aware, the Super Student Club has Focus Skills and My Pledge that we would like students to memorize. Could you please help your child to learn all the skills and the pledge? We feel it is very important that the students learn the skills and make the pledge a part of their student life.

How can you help?
Please go over the Focus Skills and the Pledge with your child. He/she will have to learn and do these skills every day. Please support your child's teacher and sign this permission slip so they can join the Super Student Club. We believe that any student can be a Super Student. It is all about a super attitude! Please call us at the school if you have any other questions.

★ Super Student Focus Skills

1. I will listen, obey, and trust my teacher.
2. I will raise my hand to speak.
3. I will think along with the speaker.
4. I will be prepared for my work.
5. I will give my best.
6. I will finish all my work.
7. I will work out problems with others.
8. I will have a positive, healthy attitude.

★ My Pledge

My attitude is the only thing I can control in life. I can choose to be happy or sad, helpful or hurtful. I can choose to be a winner in school. My attitude is reflected in these Super Student FOCUS Skills. I will read these Focus Skills every day. I will practice these skills to show I am a winner. People will see me doing these skills and good things will happen to me! As I focus on these skills, I will feel happy inside. Being GOOD is good for me! I really want to be a winner in school.

RETURN TO TEACHER
I promise to teach the Super Student Focus Skills and My Pledge to my children and will see that he/she memorizes these important facts.

Child's name_____

Teacher_____ Grade_____

Parent Signature_____

© Youthlight, Inc.

The SUPER STUDENT Program
LEADER'S GUIDE FOR GRADES 4-5

Rationale

The fourth and fifth grades in school are filled with independent and group learning. For the most part, the students in these grades have the basic academic skills necessary for survival in the real world. Students can read, write, speak, and handle the basic math skills that the world demands in everyday situations. By now they have developed social relationships and are fully aware of who is winning in school and who is not. Some students have been retained once or twice, and some have been in special education programs for quite a while.

If this is the first year of The Super Student Program for your school, the students in your class will not have heard about 'winning in school' or the survival skills that all Super Students use. In other words, this program is new to them and to you. If your school adopts the program, the years that follow will be much easier because the students will have experienced the concepts and skills in the previous grades.

Each succeeding year will be that much easier because everyone will be speaking the same language, having had the program in the lower grades. Hopefully, by that time, your celebration/recognition awards program will be in sync with the Super Student Club. At that point in time, the program will give your school some serious academic advantages.

Regardless, as you start this year with your class, believe that they are yours to mold. Nurture these skills and they grow. Celebrate them and they remain. These skills will become the survival tool kit for your students as they progress through the rest of their schooling. They will, with practice, become habitual for most students.

It is then that they will feel that they are winning. Winning in school is one of the most important games in which they will engage in. The skills identified in the Super Student Program are the skills that winners use in class to make school the most profitable setting possible. It will teach them to be responsible for their own learning and how to be a life-long learner.

Introduction for Grades 4 and 5

Teacher/Counselor says: "Today class, we are going to begin a new adventure. I am starting a club and would like everyone to join! Our club will do exciting projects and each of its members will learn how to win and be happy in school. I will teach anyone the skills necessary to win in school. My problem is that I can't make you join. I would like everyone to be in the club, but I can't make you be in it. It is a choice that you will have to make for yourself. I would like to tell you about the club and what a Super Student is. Then, after you have heard all about the program, I will invite you to sign up to be a member. Would you like to hear more about our club and what you have to do to be a member? Good! Let's start!"

I have a story for you that will start our program. It is called, "The Old Man."

Super Student Story #3: This story will be read to students in a group situation. If they can sit on a carpet or the floor in front of you, it would be best. A community circle and family atmosphere is recommended.

The Old Man

147

The Storm

Mark and Joel were bored. They were looking for something exciting to do. They turned off the TV and ran outside into the forest to be alone in the fort that they had built. As they ran through the woods, Blaze, their English setter joined them.

The fort had helped them many times before. It was a place of refuge and solitude. It allowed them to think and imagine. Many times they would just sit quietly and listen to the sounds of the forest. It seemed to speak to them.

The fort had been built of sticks about two inches in diameter and woven together with jute cord. The roof was made of bark. It was sturdy and could weather a storm. The fort stood at the top of a bluff that overlooked a beautiful valley. Pine trees abounded at the back of the fort.

The boys loved nature and would rather spend time outside camping in the forest than inside any day. Often they would spend the

The Storm (cont.)

night in the woods and enjoy the night sounds and smells. It was at times like that they felt like they were most in tune with nature.

They glanced at Blaze who was looking into the valley from the bluff. Something had caught his attention, and he was fixed on a spot down below. When something alerted Blaze's hunting instincts, he would freeze in a magnificent pose that brought everything to a halt. He was a beautiful dog with a massive head and sparkling eyes. His tail was dark with long flag-like hair. His coat was mostly black that seemed to glisten in the sunlight. Blaze's leg's also had feathered hair. These legs were attached to broad muscular shoulders made so by hours upon hours of running with Mark and Joel through the woods. Frozen in this pose, Blaze's silhouette was a living statue.

Mark broke the silence. "Joel, look at that beautiful eagle!" Sure enough, a large American bald eagle was circling overhead.

LESSON 1 — The Storm (cont.)

"Awesome!" replied Joel.

Mark said, "Have you heard about the new Super Student Program they are starting at school?"

Mark and Joel attended Green Sea Floyds Elementary School in South Carolina. Mark was in the fifth grade and Joel was in the third grade. Neither of the boys was doing well in school, and it secretly bothered them. They knew school was important, but they just couldn't figure out how to win at it. Something about school had been nagging at both of them.

"Super Student Program? What's that?" Joel replied.

"It's a program that awards good students Gold, Silver and Bronze awards for being super in school," said Mark.

"Fat chance for me to be a winner! I don't like school," replied Joel.

"I don't think most of the kids at the school know how to win that award. I know I don't! A lot of kids might want to do better, but they don't know how!" said Mark.

"Sounds like a lot of work. I'm not interested," remarked Joel.

"Let's run back. Mom said that she wanted us to go to the store to purchase some things. Come on, Blaze. Let's move!"

The boys and Blaze took off for home. It was late afternoon when they ran into the house. Their mom was making an apple pie.

"Boys, I need you to go to the store to buy some things for this pie. I'm out of sugar and cinnamon. Take Blaze. That will give

The Storm (cont.)

him a good run. Hurry and don't dilly dally.

Mark put the money in his pocket and both boys ran out of the house into the woods with Blaze following.

The boys loved to run in the woods with Blaze. He was completely different in the woods than he was in the house. Sometimes Blaze would just take off. The smells and sounds of the forest awoke something deep inside of him. He would hear a sound or smell the scent of a bird with his great nose. He was trained and bred to pick up on these things. Then, he would be off! He was almost unstoppable as he worked the forest and its smells.

Today, he was right on the trail with the boys as they jogged to the store on the opposite side of the big woods. The boys knew the way and in a short time they could see the outline of the country store through the trees.

The Storm (cont.)

Blaze was the first to arrive and waited on the porch as the boys went in to pick up the supplies.

"Hello, Mrs. Ashcroft, we need some sugar and cinnamon for mom's pie," said Joel.

"Pie, what kind of pie?" asked Mrs. Ashcroft.

"Apple!" said Mark. "My favorite!"

"Well, if you have any left over, bring some back to me," said Mrs. Ashcroft, smiling as she grabbed the sugar and cinnamon and placed them in a brown paper bag.

Mrs. Ashcroft was a kindly woman to whom the boys always enjoyed talking. She always had a loving smile that would put the boys at ease. "That will be $5.59."

The Storm (cont.)

Mark handed Mrs. Ashcroft six dollars, grabbed the paper bag, and placed it in his sack. Mrs. Ashcroft handed Mark his change.

"Thanks, Mrs. Ashcroft," said Joel.

Mrs. Ashcroft walked out onto the porch with the boys. "Boys, you had better move on. That sky is getting darker and darker by the minute. There is going to be a storm."

Mrs. Ashcroft was right. The sky had changed since they had left home. The wind was now blowing leaves and debris into the air.

"We have to go," said Mark.

As both boys ran off the porch, Blaze took off into the forest. The boys didn't know if he had seen a bird or a deer, but they saw Blaze jump a big log, and he was gone!

"Quick, Joel, follow me!" Mark jumped the same log and headed off in the opposite direction of home.

"We have to get him!" said Mark.

Blaze could run. When he was in one of these moods, he was almost unstoppable. Soon the boys were heading down hills and through woods that they had never explored during their many walks with their dad.

As they ran through one field, they noticed that the storm was quickly moving toward them. The wind was blowing overhead and the thunder was booming. The combination was starting to scare them. Then, the rain started falling. It fell in big drops that seemed to pound the forest floor. Blaze was nowhere in sight.

The Storm (cont.)

"Where are we?" said Joel, trying to yell over the storm.

"I don't know! Let's find some shelter!" said Mark. "Darkness is coming and we're lost!"

As the boys ran from the field, they could see an old house at the edge of the forest. It was an old English Tudor style home that looked like something out of a Charles Dickens novel.

The rain was now beating on them, and they were soaked to the bone. It was the lightening, however, that concerned them most. They had heard of people being hit and killed by it. They ran up to the house and knocked on a large wooden door.

End of session #1

GRADES 4-5 LEADER'S GUIDE (CONT.)

Lesson 1 Questions

- What do you think of the boy's adventure so far?
- What would you have done if you were caught in a storm like the one that overtook the boys?
- Could the boys have done something differently than go to a house they were not familiar with during this storm?

Teachers: At the end of the day send home the parent permission sheet for the Super Student Program. This is to inform the parents of the program and secure them as partners. Go to the Black line masters and use the second through fifth grade letter that is prepared for you. It is recommended highly that you read it with your students at the end of the day before they take it home.

Are you a Super Student?

This is a quick yes or no questionnaire that starts to get your students thinking about the Focus Skills and challenging them to think about their own personal responsibility for their learning. You can do this in many ways. Students can fill it out as a group and you can review it privately or they can fill it out and share with a partner and then have you look it over privately. You can continue to use this activity throughout the year at various times.

The Survival Kit

The door had a huge iron knocker that had a distinctive eagle design on it. Mark grabbed the knocker and pounded on the door over and over again. After what seemed like an eternity, the door slowly opened with a creaking sound. An old man with a friendly face peered on the other side of the door.

"Yes, can I help you?"

Mark spoke up, "The storm is coming and we are lost. Can you help us?"

"Yes, yes, come in and dry off," said the old man. "You boys will catch your death!"

The boys hesitated. Their parents had warned them to be cautious of strangers. Normally, the boys would not have entered the strange house, but the storm was so fierce and the old man seemed helpful and friendly. Perhaps they could use the phone. Because of the storm and because they were lost, they felt they had no choice.

As the boys came in they noticed a beautiful room with wooden paneled walls, beautiful furniture and pictures of nature scenes. At the far end of the room, a large fireplace stood with a warm roaring fire that seemed to make the room glow a golden color. It was warm and cheery. It was quite comfortable and quite a relief from the raging storm.

The old man had an interesting face. It was rough, tan, and weathered, but he had a gentle, loving smile. His whole face seemed to light up as he spoke. Mark guessed it was his eyes that seemed to sparkle as he talked that made them feel calm and secure. He was very bent over. The boys noticed that he used a cane as he moved further into the house.

The Survival Kit (cont.)

The old man spoke first, "Boys, you will be safe here. The storm is very bad so spend some time here with me by the fire and dry out until the storm ends. Then, I will see you home. The old man grabbed two blankets that were lying on a large chair in the foyer.

"Yes, thank you. Can we call home?" asked Joel. They took off their soaked shirts and wrapped the soft blankets around their shoulders.

"I don't have a phone, boys," replied the old man. "But I do think I have what you have been looking for!"

"Looking for?" replied Mark.

"First, pardon my manners. My name is Mr. Frost and this is Dogwood Acres."

"Dogwood Acres? I never heard of it!" said Mark.

© Youthlight, Inc.

The Survival Kit (cont.)

"Of course," replied the old man. "This is quite far out in the big woods, you know. The old man paused and seemed to be thinking. "I know this is hard to believe, but I think I can help you both."

"You have helped us already!" said Joel.

"No, I don't mean about the storm, Mark and Joel. I mean about school."

There was silence except for the boom of thunder that had just shaken the house. The boys looked at each other in surprise. The old man seemed so kind and spoke with such a soft gentle voice.

"How do you know that we need help?" replied Mark. "And how do you know our names?"

"Oh, I know many things, but that's not important. You have been asking some very important questions about school. What is important is that you find your answers!"

The boys looked at each other in awe! Who is this guy, thought Mark?

"Come and sit down for a while boys, until the storm passes. I will make sure you get home safely when it is over." Two large comfortable sofas stood in front of the fire. The boys sat down in one of them.

Mr. Frost grabbed a large letterbox that looked like a chest. On the top of the chest the words **SURVIVAL KIT** were carved into the wood. He opened the box lid and grabbed out a large letter with a white wax seal that held the letter closed. The seal had a beautiful imprint of an American bald eagle.

The Survival Kit (cont.)

"Do you want to know the secrets to being a winner in school?"

"School?" said Mark surprised at the question.

"Yes, in school and in life also," said the old man.

"Yea, I guess so," said Mark as he glanced over to Joel and saw him smiling.

"Good. First, you must really want to be a Super Student!"

"Super Student?" said Mark.

"Boys, I know you have been feeling badly about school, and this night might be the chance for you to change that. You know, nothing happens by accident. There is a purpose in everything that happens to us."

This was a phrase that the boys had heard often from their mom and dad. Their mom and dad both believed that God had a

© Youthlight, Inc.

The Survival Kit (cont.)

special purpose for everyone's life and that nothing happened by accident. The boys didn't know how this old man knew this, but he was right. They had not felt right about school. They wanted to do well in school but they didn't know how or where to start. Also, for Mark, it just didn't seem cool. And Joel usually followed Mark's lead.

Something felt strange about this whole day. Time in this house seemed to stand still. Were they dreaming? They felt that they were somehow destined to be here in this old home during the storm and with this strange, kind old man. He seemed to know all about them and was willing to help. They felt that he somehow believed in them. They trusted him. They felt encouraged.

The boys looked at each other. Then, they glanced outside the large window where the rain was beating on the glass. The thunder was still booming overhead. It was now pitch black outside except for the constant lighting that was flashing. What did they

The Survival Kit (cont.)

have to lose? They couldn't run back out into the storm. The weather was still raging outside. They felt safe and somewhat interested in this kind old man. Perhaps, if they would humor him and talk awhile, the storm would pass.

"So do you want to be winners in school? Do you believe you can?" asked the man.

"Yes, sure we do!" said Mark, more intrigued than ever.

"Yes," said Joel smiling as he watched Mark's face to see what he was thinking.

"If you do not believe that you can, the magic will not work!" said the old man.

"Magic?" said Joel looking at his brother sideways.

"Yes, magic," remarked the old man.

"We don't know where to begin. What does it take to be a winner?" said Joel.

"First, you must believe you can be. Then, you need the Magic Eight Skills."

"The Magic Eight?" said Mark.

"The Magic Eight are skills that, if students focus on them, will

© Youthlight, Inc.

The Survival Kit (cont.)

bring them great rewards and happiness in school. These are the skills or things that all good students use to be successful. They have never been written down until now. I have eight letters that have magic wax seals. But, remember the magic does not work unless the student wants to be a Super Student! Each of these letters contains one of the secrets."

This old man seemed kind enough, even though he seems to be a little strange thought Mark. We'll just play along until the storm stops. He seems harmless enough. The fire felt good and Mark noticed that they were starting to dry out. How does he know so much about us? Mark could not remove that thought from his head. Who is this old man and what does he want from us?

End of session#2

GRADES 4-5 LEADER'S GUIDE (CONT.)

Lesson 2 Questions

Ask your students these questions. Have a good discussion.

- What do think of Mark and Joel's adventure so far?
- Describe the old man.
- What do you think the words **SURVIVAL KIT** meant on the top of the chest?
- Why do you think the old man told the boys that a student needs to want to be a Super Student to receive the magic of the skills?
- Why do you think Mark and Joel wanted to believe?
- Why do they trust the old man?
- What would you have done if you were in the boys' place?

Super Student Crossword Puzzle for The Old Man

This activity is a lot of fun for your students. Don't miss it! See the Black line masters for the black line master for this exciting crossword puzzle.

The Super Student True or False Test

This is a quick true or false questionnaire that starts to get your students thinking about the Focus Skills and challenges them to think about their own personal responsibility for their learning. You can do this in many ways. Students can fill it out as a group and you can review it privately or they can fill it out and share with a partner and then have you look it over privately. You can continue to use this activity throughout the year at various times.

© Youthlight, Inc.

The White Seal

"Break the white wax seal on the letter," said the old man.

Mark grabbed the letter and used his finger to break open the white seal. He could hardly wait to open the letter. In large letters were the words, **"I WILL LISTEN, OBEY, AND TRUST MY TEACHER."**

"Read it out loud. I see you have some belief because you were able to break the seal," said Mr. Frost. The boys recited it together. "This is the first and most important skill that all Super Students use in class every day," said the man.

"That's hard to do!" replied Mark.

"Of course it is. But you must stay focused. Why do you go to school?"

The White Seal (cont.)

"To learn, I guess," said Mark.

"That's right. School is a place for you to prepare yourself. Teachers are your friends. They care about their students and want them to learn the work and do well in class."

"You don't know my teacher!" said Joel. "She's mean."

Mr. Frost laughed. The laughter seemed to melt any of the fears that the boys had about the old man. It was such a warm and sincere laugh.

"All that teachers are trying to do is their jobs. Of course, they give you work and discipline you when you do something wrong so you will learn. If a teacher is not correcting you when you are wrong, something is wrong with that teacher!" The old man took a deep breath and sighed.

"Some of the teachers you will like. Some you will not like. He/she wants you to learn all the important things in this grade level so you will not be fooled or tricked in the world. You don't think you will like everyone you work for when you have a job do you? Learning to listen, obey and trust those people who are over you is very important."

"A Super Student listens to every word his/her teacher says and obeys every time he/she asks you to do something. They do it because they know the teacher is directing their school life."

"Even if you don't want to listen?" asked Joel.

"Yes, Joel. Even then. Making yourself do the right thing, even when you don't want to, is the way to develop your character. A funny thing happens when we listen when we don't want to. We

LESSON 3 — The White Seal (cont.)

take control over our life and feelings. We become the boss and we become responsible."

Mark and Joel knew the old man was telling the truth. They nodded their heads in agreement. Joel remembered one time when he did not want to finish some work the teacher had given him. He had to push the bad feelings down and forced himself to do what was right. Sometimes, however, he didn't do the work and that bad feeling would stay with him all day long. He would try to hide it, but he couldn't run away from it.

"When you are selfish, you know in your heart that you are wrong. That's exactly how you are behaving when you want your own way in school. You come to school to learn from the teacher. She is not learning from you.

Trusting your teacher to lead you in school is what being a student is all about! You have to be the boss over your mind and your body!" said the old man. "You're in control of your attitude. It is the only thing you can control!"

Joel and Mark looked at each other. They knew they were guilty of this. They looked at school as a prison and the teacher as a jail warden. Maybe, they had it wrong. Mr. Frost was saying that school was an opportunity and a blessing. He believed that teachers were there to help nurture them and help them grow. Maybe, how you look at things really does matter! They could see that is could be the most important skill of all. Maybe, this old man had something to say. Could it be that they had it all wrong?

End of session #3

GRADES 4-5 LEADER'S GUIDE (CONT.)

Lesson 3 Questions

- What is the first Super Student skill?
- Why is it difficult to do?
- Why is it important?
- Why do all of us dislike being told what to do?
- What did the old man mean when he said, "You must be the boss over your body and mind"?
- What did he mean when he said, "You're in control of your attitude!"
- What does attitude mean?
- How is your attitude important in school and in life?

To The Teacher

You can tell your students what listening and obeying means to you. Tell them what you are trying to accomplish by having them obey and trust you.

Super Student Skill Sheet #1
I WILL LISTEN, OBEY AND TRUST MY TEACHER.

Have your students work on this later in the day. After the worksheet is finished and shared, send these worksheets home to be signed. When they return, you can save these worksheets (there are eight of them) in a personal Super Student folder that at the end of the story will go home with the Super Student membership card and certificate.

The Super Formula

Let your students read this first quietly and then let various students read the letters and their meaning. Conduct a good discussion about the letter meanings. They could then each pick a letter and draw a picture or a scene that depicts the letter meaning. Under the picture they can write a short description of what the letter has to do with their improvement as a student.

Super Student Definitions for Listen, Obey, and Trust

Have your students answer these questions privately first and then have a sharing time. It will be interesting to see what they have to say! (See blackline masters at the end of this section for grades 4-5).

© Youthlight, Inc.

The Yellow Seal

"Ok," said Mark. "You have my attention now! What about the next letter?" For some reason, Mark seemed more interested in what the old man had to say. Maybe it was the storm or the warmth of the old man's voice and house, but Mark felt a mystery about what the old man was saying.

The old man reached in the chest and brought out the second letter. It was large and had a yellow seal on it. Joel reached for it and broke the seal. He then pulled out the second letter to read. In large yellow letters it said, **"I WILL RAISE MY HAND TO SPEAK."**

"I guess we're getting down to what Super Students do to show that they are super," stated Joel.

"This skill, like all the others, is very important. In school," said the old man, "teachers deal with groups of students. It is bad manners to speak when someone else is speaking. If everyone is speaking, no one hears. Good students know this and they control themselves when they are in a group discussion."

Mark remarked, "I have a boy in my class who is always calling out and cutting up in class. He is a big show off who is always trying to attract everyone's attention."

The old man smiled, "He doesn't sound like a Super Student!"

"No. He is always being sent out of class to the principal's office. Then his parents come in to talk to the principal and he goes home for two or three days."

"Do you think that he is winning in school?" replied the old man.

"Not really! He's failing in school and will probably have to

The Yellow Seal (cont.)

repeat the grade. The funny thing is that I think he is pretty smart!"

"That's my point!" said the old man. "Now, do you really think that boy is happy?" The boys looked at each other with sad and serious faces. The old man noticed this exchange of glances and went on.

"The teacher controls the discussion in class. That's his/her job. When you raise your hand and continue to show manners and respect in class even when other students continue to be disrespectful, you are winning in school."

Mark asked, "How can you be good when other kids tease and make fun of you for trying to be a good student? A lot of kids think it's not cool to be good in school and make good grades. It's hard to take it every day."

The Yellow Seal (cont.)

Mr. Frost paused for a moment to feel the full weight of what Mark had just said. He knew all along that Mark was the student he had just described.

Then he asked, "Who cares about you, Mark? Who loves you?"

"What do you mean?" inquired Mark.

"Let's get this straight," replied the old man. "You guys have just been polite to agree with me up to this point. Are you ready to be real and genuine?

Your relatives, parents, real friends, and teachers care about you. They will be with you all through your life. Do you think that the kids that tease you are your real friends? Do you think that they care about you when you go to the principal's office, and you are waiting for your parents to come to school? If you are trying to impress these kids who try to lead you into trouble and enjoy it when you are in trouble, you're playing to the wrong audience."

"Audience?" asked Mark.

"Yes, you are trying to impress the wrong group! You should be caring more about the people who love you. Do you think that your relatives enjoy coming into the school to talk to the principal about your bad behavior? Do you think you are making the people who care about you proud?"

Mark and Joel put their heads down. The things that the old man said had struck deeply. It had taken the breath out of them!

They loved their mom and dad and other relatives too. When they had days like the old man described, they had never realized how much they were hurting the people that loved them. Mark

The Yellow Seal (cont.)

remembered one time he had caught his mom crying in her room after he had been sent home. Mark and Joel felt ashamed.

The old man sensed this and continued, "Mark, Joel, remember I told you that you have to want to be a Super Student in order to unlock the magic."

"Yes," they said.

"Well, it is decision time! You have been with me only halfway up until now. I need a commitment from both of you to go further." The boys knew what the old man meant.

"You have to have a reason to be a Super Student. It could be just because it is good for you and that it will make you happy. Or, it could be because it is good for you and those you love. But to change your life, you must have a reason, and it has to be important to you."

At that moment, the boys knew which audience that they would play to from now on. They were not going to hurt their parents or their relatives any more. They were choosing to become Super Students! And they wouldn't care about what the other students or people thought anymore.

End of session # 4

GRADES 4-5 LEADER'S GUIDE (CONT.)

Lesson 4 Questions

- What do you think of the story so far?
- What big decision did the boys make at this point? Why?
- What was Mark's reason for not being a Super Student?
- How did the old man answer him?
- Why should we raise our hands in class?
- Why is it as important to ask questions as to answer questions?
- Has anyone here made a decision about being a Super Student? If you would like to talk to me after this lesson, please let me know.

Teacher

Super Student Skill Sheet #2
I WILL RAISE MY HAND TO SPEAK.

Have your students work on this later in the day. After the worksheet is finished and shared, send these worksheets home to be signed. When they return, you can save these worksheets (there are eight of them) in a personal Super Student folder that at the end of the story will go home with the Super Student membership card and certificate.

Try to think of your teacher like this: The Super Student Way

Have your students take turns reading this after they read it quietly to themselves. Let them then break into pairs and discuss two numbers each with each other. Ask them to answer this question, "Is this true? Why?" Then they can share in the total group what their neighbor shared with them.

Asking & Answering Questions – Check It Out!

This is an interesting activity that is an eye opener. It answers the question, "Do I raise my hand a lot to answer or ask questions?" It will tell your students something about their level of participation. I would do this only for a day for practical reasons. You can get a summary at the end of the day. (See black line masters at the end of this section for grades 4-5)

The Orange Seal

"Would you boys like a cup of hot cocoa?" inquired the old man. The words woke the boys out of the deep thoughts that they had about the decision they had just made. Somehow the decision to change had energized them. They felt inspired and ready to start over again, just like on the first day of school, thought Mark.

"Yes, I would love it," replied Mark.

"Great," Joel chimed in. As the old man stood up to get the hot cocoa, the boys noticed that the storm was still pounding outside. We'll probably have to boat home by the time morning comes, thought Joel. Sitting so close to the warm fire had dried their clothing and the thought of a nice cup of hot cocoa was inviting.

As Mr. Frost handed each of the boys a cup of hot cocoa, he slipped Joel the third letter. He could sense that they had made the commitment to continue. The letter was sealed with a bright orange wax seal. As Joel opened the seal, the boys knew they would be looking at these magic skills a little differently now.

Joel handed the letter to Mark. The note was written in dark orange letters. It said, **"I WILL THINK ALONG WITH THE SPEAKER"**.

"What do you think that means?" inquired the old man.

"Oh, I think I know," said Mark. "When anyone is speaking in class, you must listen, really listen, to what they are saying. You should turn your head toward them and really follow what they are trying to say to everyone."

"Yes, that's right!" said Joel. "You will be learning from others as well as the teacher! I know a lot of kids who don't do that."

The Orange Seal (cont.)

"Well, they are losing and missing out in school," said the old man.

"Maybe we could change all that," suggested Joel.

"What do you mean?" asked Mark.

"Maybe we could make it cool to be a Super Student and start a Club!" said Joel. This idea struck Mark. Mark was popular in school. He was an athlete, and no one pushed him around very much. If he would be willing to be in a Super Student Club, he knew he could find others to follow his lead.

LESSON 5

The Orange Seal (cont.)

The old man knew this as he said, "Now you are starting to think about others, Mark. I can see that you are really taking this seriously."

It is about time I take something seriously besides cutting up in class, thought Mark. Of all the people he had hurt, he knew he had hurt his mom most of all. She had always been full of love, and Mark knew his school behavior had meant the most to her. I don't care what others kids think anymore. I'm doing the right thing from now on! I'm not letting my mom and dad go through this punishment and pain anymore because of my selfishness.

"The Super Student Club sounds great!" said Joel. Mark knew he had his first member when Joel said that. His brother would follow anything he would do because Joel looked up to him so much. Mark realized that he had been failing his brother. He loved his brother very much, and he had been setting the wrong example. "This stuff is going to stop!" Mark vowed silently.

"Manners and respect have a lot to do with being a Super Student," remarked the old man. The teacher notices all of this in class. He/she knows if you have manners and respect and if you are trying to improve yourself. You can't fool him/her. In fact, you can't fool the other students in your class either. They know all about you."

Well, they're going to see a new me, thought Mark as he sipped the hot cocoa.

"Tell us a little more about thinking along with the speaker, Mr. Frost."

The old man smiled. "What did I say? Why are you smiling?" questioned Mark.

The Orange Seal (cont.)

"You just used an important skill," remarked the old man.

"I did?" said Mark. "You asked a question that pertained to what we were talking about. Asking good questions is very important for Super Students. It allows them to stretch their minds. They grow smarter! But they have to be following the speaker's thoughts to ask good questions. In fact, it is better to ask questions than to have all the answers. Asking shows the teacher that you are thinking creatively. It also shows that you are tuned in to the learning."

The old man continued, "There's one more thing concerning answering and asking questions. Even if the teacher does not pick you to answer a question, remember that he/she sees your hand. You don't have to be picked to answer every question for the teacher to see that you are trying to participate. So, think along with the speaker by raising your hand to ask or answer ques-

LESSON 5

The Orange Seal (cont.)

tions, use good body language and use your good manners in a group. All Super Students know these secrets."

"What is body language"? Mark asked.

"Body language is the way you sit, how your eyes follow the speaker, and the respect that you give the speaker with your body. It is the way you speak to people without using your mouth. It is extremely important in communication. Your teacher is aware of it all the time," The old man said.

"Sounds like a lot to learn!" said Joel.

"Not really," said the old man. "It becomes a good habit. After a while, you won't even need to think about it. But you will need to practice it everyday so it becomes a habit! Mark, do you think about what to do with your hands and feet when you are running the football?"

" No, of course not! I just run. It's all sort of natural."

"Exactly," said Mr. Frost as he smiled. The two boys looked at each other. How was it that they could get caught in a storm and wind up in this old man's house? He was so good and wise. Mark felt lucky and blessed.

Where was this all going? Mom and dad must be looking for them by now. Although, it seemed like they had just arrived, Mark wondered what time it was as he peered around the room. He looked around the room again, but he couldn't locate a clock. Time seemed to have stopped.

End of session #5

© Youthlight, Inc.

GRADES 4-5 LEADER'S GUIDE (CONT.)

Lesson 5 Questions

- What does thinking along with the speaker mean?
- Why is it important?
- What is body language?
- Why is it important in a group discussion?
- Why did the old man consider Mark a Super Student?
- Why is Mark changing his attitude?
- What did the old man say about asking good questions?
- What did he mean when he said, "This will become a good habit after awhile"?

Teacher

Super Student Skill Sheet #3
I WILL THINK ALONG WITH THE SPEAKER

Have your students work on this later in the day. After the worksheet is finished and shared, send these worksheets home to be signed. When they return, you can save these worksheets (there are eight of them) in a personal Super Student folder that at the end of the story will go home with the Super Student membership card and certificate.

Super Student Survey

This is a personal survey and touches some personal issues about not being a good student. Collect this only if the students want to let you read it. You will be surprised to see how many will share it with you if you handle it this way.

The Green Seal

The fourth seal was green. The old man handed the envelope to Mark who broke the seal, pulled the letter out and read, **"I WILL BE PREPARED FOR ALL MY WORK."**

"Sounds important!" said Joel. Mark could see that Joel was getting into this Super Student stuff. That seemed like a miracle in itself!

"Being prepared with your books, papers, pencils, and notepads not only helps you to be ready to learn, but also tells the teacher that you are serious about your job."

The Green Seal (cont.)

"Job?" asked Joel.

"Yes, job," said the old man. "Going to school is the job that students do. Your relatives have jobs that they go to every day.

"Yes, but they are paid for their work," Joel objected.

Mr. Frost countered, "So are students! It's called a report card."

"But that's not money!" said Mark.

"No, it isn't yet. But it will be later in life when you change reading, writing, math, science, and social studies into a job that pays real money.

A lot of kids don't understand that they are learning skills and knowledge that will pay them later in their future jobs. Their effort really does pay off! In today's world, if you don't know very much, or can't do very much, you aren't paid very much! People are not going to pay you for work that you can't do. So, being prepared for your work in school becomes a Super Student skill because it gets you ready to do your job."

End of session #6

GRADES 4-5 LEADER'S GUIDE (CONT.)

Lesson 6 Questions

- What are some of the materials you need to have to be prepared for your work? Why?
- How is school like a job?
- What do employers think of workers who are not ready for their work for the day?
- What are some jobs that require that you must be ready each day for your work?

Teacher

Super Student Skill Sheet #4
I WILL BE PREPARED FOR MY WORK

Have your students work on this later in the day. After the worksheet is finished and shared, send these worksheets home to be signed. When they return, you can save these worksheets (there are eight of them) in a personal Super Student folder that at the end of the story will go home with the Super Student membership card and certificate.

The Top Ten Facts About Being a Super Students

Again, this is a read quietly and share activity. Have your students read these ten facts and then pair up and share three of their favorites. Bring the group back to share what their partner thought.

© Youthlight, Inc.

The Brown Seal

The fifth letter was sealed with a double brown wax seal. It had to be handled carefully so as to not tear the parchment.

"Why does this letter have a double seal?" asked Mark.

"Because this skill is so important and precious," said the old man.

The old man handed Mark a letter opener to carefully cut through the double wax seal. In brown writing the boys read the words, **"I WILL GIVE MY BEST."**

"This is skill number five," said the old man. "Do you know why it is important?"

"You owe it to many people to do your best. Your family, friends, and community are all counting on you when you are in school. You are the future! But do you know to whom you owe the most?"

The Brown Seal (cont.)

"No, who?" asked Joel.

"Yourself," said the old man. You go through this life only once. When you are in school you have a chance to become anything you want to be. You are preparing yourself for your and your family's future. And you have the time right now."

"Time?" said Mark.

"Yes, time is a very precious item. You don't have extra time. It's precious. Now is your time to prepare. We never know how much time we have, so we shouldn't waste it. You need to be busy now, taking advantage of the time you have to study and learn all you can. Your teachers, counselors, and principals are all there. They are willing and able to help you, but you will need to be the one to do the work. No one will do it for you. When you don't give your best, you cheat yourself, and you lose in school. Super Students push themselves. They give their best!"

The old man seemed to be serious as he said this. It was almost as if he was running out of time and he was trying to give great importance to everything he was saying. The boys glanced at each other and nodded as if to say, you are telling the truth, Mr. Frost!

End of session #7

GRADES 4-5 LEADER'S GUIDE (CONT.)

Lesson 7 Questions

- What does being prepared for your work mean?
- What did the old man mean when he said, "School is like a job."
- How does school prepare you for your future career?
- What does 'giving your best' mean?
- Why is it important?
- Why is time important?
- To whom do you owe hard work? Why?
- Why do you think that the old man was so serious?

Teacher

Super Student Skill Sheet #5
I WILL GIVE MY BEST.

Have your students work on this later in the day. After the worksheet is finished and shared, send these worksheets home to be signed. When they return, you can save these worksheets (there are eight of them) in a personal Super Student folder that at the end of the story will go home with the Super Student membership card and certificate.

12 Tips for Raising Your Grades

Have your students read these out loud in a group. Pass out a clean sheet of paper and have them create a small symbol or cartoon to depict the meaning of each tip. The results should be interesting. If it turns out well, display them in the room or hallway.

LESSON 8

The Red Seal

The sixth letter had a red wax seal on it. Joel reached in the box and grabbed it tightly.

"We are almost finished," said Joel. "You have been very helpful, Mr. Frost." Joel could see that only two letters remained in the box. He handed the letter to Mark. As he did, he noticed writing in red ink on the outside of the letter. "Can you read the writing, Mark?"

It says, "Beat the work. Don't let the work beat you!"

"What in the world does that mean?" asked Joel.

"Find out by opening the letter," said the old man. Mark broke the red seal and pulled out the letter. It said, **"I WILL FINISH ALL MY WORK."**

"This is the sixth skill," said the old man.

"Does it mean homework?" asked Joel.

"It means all work that the teacher gives you. Classwork, homework, papers, projects and all assignments are included.

Everything the teacher gives you to do. Trust your teacher. Don't let the work beat you!"

"Why do you say it like that?" asked Joel.

"Because when you don't finish the work that your teacher gives you, the work just beats you! You lose!" remarked the man.

"Do you mean it's like a game?" asked Mark.

© Youthlight, Inc.

The Red Seal (cont.)

"If it is a game, school is the most important game that you will ever play. If you lose at school it will hurt a lot of people, but, mostly, it will hurt you."

Mark thought about all the times that he did not finish his work and all the people he had hurt, including his teachers. How much had he lost? Look at all he had missed! No more, he

The Red Seal (cont.)

thought. He knew it wouldn't be easy, but he promised to make it up. This club will help and so will the Super Student Program. He had almost forgotten! It was starting at the school. That would be a good goal. He vowed to earn at least a Bronze and then he would shoot for Silver and Gold awards. Just wait.

The old man continued, "If you don't understand the work and it's hard to finish, go to your teacher for help. Don't keep it inside. Ask for help! Super Students are not afraid if they don't know it all. They look for people to help them if they are having a problem. Help is all around you. Teachers, counselors, and principals want to help students. That's why they work in schools. So ask for help, then finish all your work and give your best every time."

"All these skills seem to work together!" said Joel.

"Now you're getting it!" said the old man smiling. He was right. The boys were getting it. They didn't feel on the outside any more. They were beginning to feel that they had the answers and knew the way to win at school. They felt differently inside. They had control and it felt good. And they would make it cool to be in the club. Just wait and see!

End of session #8

© Youthlight, Inc.

GRADES 4-5 LEADER'S GUIDE (CONT.)

Lesson 8 Questions
- What does 'beat the work' mean?
- What should you do if you are having problems with schoolwork?
- Who can help you with problems in school?
- The way you finish homework says what about your character?
- Why do you think that someone who finishes his work would be a good person to hire for a job?
- What did the old man mean when he said, "School is the most important game you will ever play."?
- What did Joel mean when he said, "All of these skills work together!"?
- Mark set a goal during this session. What was it? Why is goal setting important?
- Do you have any goals?

Teacher

Super Student Skill Sheet #6
I WILL FINISH ALL MY WORK

Have your students work on this later in the day. After the worksheet is finished and shared, send these worksheets home to be signed. When they return, you can save these worksheets (there are eight of them) in a personal Super Student folder that at the end of the story will go home with the Super Student membership card and certificate.

Super Student Week in Review

This activity continues to challenge your students to personal look at their Super Student Skills. The more they evaluate themselves and look at their behavior against the Focus Skills the more they are training themselves to be a Super Student. Sooner or later they have to come to the conclusion that they are in charge of their behavior and success in school. You, as teacher can only teach the skills and open the door for them to change their behavior.

The Blue Seal

Mr. Frost handed the next letter to the boys. The seventh letter's wax seal seemed to be changing shades of blue. First, it would be a light blue and then change to sky blue, to darker blue and then to a deep dark blue. Finally, it would return to light blue and then repeat the color changes.

"Now, this is strange!" said Joel.

"Yeah, you don't see that every day!" remarked Mark.

"Why is it changing to different shades of blue?" asked Joel.
"It is trying to tell you something in this next skill about feeling blue." commented the old man.

"Is this a sad skill?" asked Mark.

The old man paused, "No, but it could be if you are not doing it. All the other skills deal with your work with your teacher. But school is more than that. It is about working with and around others. If you were the only student in school, it would be easier but boring. Having other students around you makes school exciting."

"And difficult!" said Mark.

Mr. Frost laughed. "That's true!"

"I would have no problem winning that Celebration Award if I was the only student in my class." said Joel. "Some of those kids are mean and distracting."

The old man smiled, "That's why this skill is so important!"

Joel picked out the note. It was written in large blue letters.

© Youthlight, Inc.

The Blue Seal (cont.)

Everyone noticed that even the ink was turning shades of blue. This must be important, he thought. The note read, **"I WILL WORK OUT PROBLEMS WITH OTHERS."**

"I knew we were going to talk about this one," said Mark.

"What does it mean?" asked Joel.

The old man said, "It means that schools do not allow fighting, hitting, yelling, and screaming. When you have a problem with

The Blue Seal (cont.)

another student, you must work it out, even if it's not your fault. Super Students can't be involved in disputes and disruptions."

"Some kids will try to lead you into trouble by getting you so mad that you lose your cool and you start a fight or say things to get back. Many times the other kids will encourage you, so they can see a fight. Some kids like trouble. I know. I've been in fights!" Mark replied.

"That's right", said the old man, "Everything you said is true, but you have to decide if you are going to play it that way."

"The kids will call you chicken if you don't fight!" said Joel. "They know how to push the right buttons so that you lose your temper!"

"What should we do, Mr. Frost?" asked Mark.

The old man could see it in the boys' faces that they were struggling with this one, so he said, "I am glad you're interested, Mark."

The old man knew Mark could take care of himself and that Mark had been in his share of fights outside of school. But he also knew that Mark never felt right after the fights.

"This problem can ruin you even if you are a pretty good student. If you want to be a Super Student, you must stay out of trouble. Here are the secrets and the magic."

Both boys leaned forward. They knew this was a big problem in school because many times students would tease or try to lead them into trouble. They wondered what to do because they felt like punching and hitting back.

The Blue Seal (cont.)

The old man spoke, "First, you need to join in with the kids who are trying to stay out of trouble. You will be surprised how much that will help! However, you will meet kids who are looking for trouble. They want you to share in their trouble and the problems they are going through. When you feel angry because of something someone said or did to you, try talking it out and working it out. If that doesn't work, then remove yourself from the area and calm down. Take three deep breaths or count backwards slowly. But remove yourself."

"Suppose they follow you and continue to drive you crazy!" asked Joel.

"Continue to move away and look for an adult to talk to about the problem."

"They'll call you chicken or baby!" Joel replied.

"Let them!" said the old man. "Are you being a chicken or being smart? You're in school. It's the wrong place to fight. You are on track to become a Super Student. They will receive their punishment. Don't you think the teachers know these kids? They do know them and they'll get caught. These kids just want you to come along on their ride out of school. Do you want to go?"

"No, not now!" said Mark. "It's not worth it!"

"Exactly!" said the old man. "So don't let them take you on the ride! You are the only one who suffers when you blow up and play their game. Listen, your relatives, teachers, counselor, and principal are the people who care about you in school."

LESSON 9
The Blue Seal (cont.)

"What about your friends?" Joel asked.

"If they are real friends, they will want you safe and out of trouble. If they want you in trouble, they're not your friends!"

Now, Mark and Joel smiled. They knew the old man was telling the truth again. They understood that kids don't lead you into trouble. You lead yourself into trouble. You are the boss over your body and your mind thought Mark. And he was right!

End of session #9

© Youthlight, Inc.

GRADES 4-5 LEADER'S GUIDE (CONT.)

Lesson 9 Questions

- Why can this problem ruin Super Students?
- What were some of the secrets that the old man shared with the boys?
- What would a true friend do if you were being bullied or teased? How could they help?
- What did the old man mean when he said, " Your teacher, counselor and principal are the only ones who care for you in school?"
- Does this problem happen here at our school? Discuss.
- What is the difference between tattling and telling a teacher if someone is bothering you? *Note:* Tattling is telling about something you are not involved in and is not dangerous or that important. Telling a teacher that you have a personal problem is OK.

Teacher

Super Student Skill Sheet #7
I WILL WORK OUT PROBLEMS WITH OTHERS.

Have your students work on this later in the day. After the worksheet is finished and shared, send these worksheets home to be signed. When they return, you can save these worksheets (there are eight of them) in a personal Super Student folder that at the end of the story will go home with the Super Student membership card and certificate.

Working Out Problems with Others

Let your students read this quietly and then pick students to read it out loud in the group. Have them choose one of the steps and write a short story about a student who did this step during a problem situation with another student. Share the stories. Have the students use the word processor and publish their short story. Display the finished work.

Super Students use "I Messages"

Have your students read the directions and numbers 1 to 5 out loud. Then, have them work the examples 1 to 5. Go over the results out loud with the class.

© Youthlight, Inc.

The Black Seal

They had reached the last letter. It had a large black seal on the seam. The storm was still blowing. Rain was still beating hard against the windowpane, and the thunder and lightning continued. This was the worst storm they had ever seen.

"More hot cocoa boys? That storm looks as if it is going to go on all night long. We'll have you home in the morning. It will be difficult to find the way in the dark in this kind of weather."

"Yes," said Mark. "More hot cocoa would be great!"

"I'll get it from the kitchen," said the old man as he slowly lifted himself from the couch.

"Oh boys, don't open the last letter until I return."

The boys looked at the box that contained the last letter. With all the discussion about the letters with the colored seals, they

The Black Seal (cont.)

had not noticed how magnificent the box was that held the magic letters. It was a beautiful red cedar box with gold hinges and a gold keyhole. On the top of the box were the words, **"SURVIVAL KIT."** It's a good title for this box, thought Mark.

"Pretty nice box, you know, Joel."

"Yeah, It's beautiful!" said Joel. "You know, Mark, we are learning a lot tonight and I am enjoying myself, but don't you think we should get on home?"

"How can we walk home in the dark with this storm going on?" questioned Mark.

The boys looked at the letters in the box that they had gone through with Mr. Frost. They had broken the white, yellow, orange, green, brown, red, and blue seals. They had learned a lot about school and Super Student skills. They would have a lot of work to do in school when they returned, but they had been changed on this stormy night. They had dealt with things about school that had been bothering them for a long time. What could the last letter hold?

They quickly reviewed their adventure, and the way they had been rescued from the storm by this friendly old man. He had been an answer to prayer. And now they were going to start a Super Student Club! Who would have guessed?

"Dad will probably have a heart attack!" said Mark. Both boys laughed.

"Dad will be proud. You know how serious he is about education!" said Joel.

The Black Seal (cont.)

The old man returned with the hot cocoa and filled the boys' cups. Mr. Frost paused for a moment. "Boys, we have come full circle. This last letter is very special to me. This last skill is like the first one. It is very important. You will notice that the seal is black. The color black is used as the color of the highest belt level in karate. It means maturity or excellence. It is a good choice for this last skill." "Please open it, Mark."

Mark used the letter opener and broke the black wax seal for the last letter. He pulled out the letter and read, **"I WILL HAVE A POSITIVE, HEALTHY, ATTITUDE."**

"A positive, healthy, attitude in school really identifies a Super Student," said the old man.

"What does attitude mean?" asked Joel.

"Attitude is the way you feel and think about things. It influences your whole life. Your attitude influences the way you act and behave. It is one of the few things in life that you have control over. But it must be developed or nurtured through your experiences. You can choose to be happy or sad, helpful or hurtful. Remember you are in control of your thinking."

"If you decide to be a winner in school, you will practice and pick up the Super Student skills that show

© Youthlight, Inc.

The Black Seal (cont.)

others that you are winning in school. This will affect your attitude. You will see yourself growing and getting better and stronger. Your positive attitude will grow. Having a positive attitude means being optimistic and thinking the best of things!"

Mark snapped his fingers and said, "I have a friend who was born with a physical handicap. He can't walk. He has to use a wheelchair. Yet, he's always happy and the kids all like him. He's a pretty good student also, especially in math. He's moved away now, and I miss him, but he taught me that I have a lot to be thankful for."

"Good story, Mark. That friend's attitude was what was shinning through. Sometimes you will fail at something or an experience may be hard to move through. Just keep on doing what is right. In other words, we all are knocked down from time to time. We just can't stay down!

Boys, you can't blame anyone for your attitude but yourself. You can take full credit for it. You control your attitude about school. Think about the good side of things. It will control your attitude."

"Do you mean like counting your blessings? Mom always says that!" said Joel.

"Exactly!" remarked the old man. "Think about all the good things that are coming your way. Always look on the bright side, even if bad things are happening. Good things will happen to you! That's a promise!"

The old man was silent for what seemed like an eternity and then said, "Boys now that we have finished at the last letter, I have a gift for you and your club."

The Black Seal (cont.)

The boys looked at each other in surprise as the old man pulled a black ribbon that held a rolled up piece of parchment. The parchment looked very old and official. He unrolled the paper and asked Mark to read it. It read:

My Pledge

My attitude is the only thing I can control in life. I can choose to be happy or sad, helpful or hurtful. I can choose to be a winner in school. My attitude is reflected in these Super Student Focus skills. I will read these Focus skills every day. I will practice these skills to show I am a winner. People will see me using these skills and good things will happen to me! As I focus on these skills, I will feel happy inside. Being good is good for me! I really want to be a winner in school.

The Black Seal (cont.)

"This can be our pledge for the club," said Mark. "Thank you, Mr. Frost!"

"It would make me happy if you used it," remarked the old man.

Mark placed the last letter and the Pledge neatly into the red cedar box and closed the lid. He yawned.

"Thank you, Mr. Frost for everything that you have done for us this evening. We will always remember this night."

The boys both yawned. " I'm getting tired and we need to return home…." The boys yawned again.

"Oh, boys, you'll return home safely. I promise. This evening has meant more to me than you can imagine." The room seemed to spin and then, all went black.

The boys awoke with the sun shinning on their faces. They were lying under a large live oak tree. It was a beautiful day! The boys looked out on a beautiful meadow. The old cottage and the old man were nowhere in sight.

"Where are we?" asked Joel.

The Black Seal (cont.)

"I don't know, but isn't that Blaze?"

"Yes!" Joel said. "Blaze! Blaze!"

Blaze, hearing his name, picked up his ears and came running toward the boys. When Blaze made it to the boys, they threw their arms around him and hugged his beautiful neck.

"Home, boy, let's move!" they said. Blaze took off and the boys followed through the forest. Soon they reached a path with which they were familiar. They knew they were on the right trail now! Soon, they could see two people coming toward them.

"It's Mom and Dad!" shouted Joel. "Mom, Dad!"

"Boys!"

"Here they are, Jane!"

Everyone met and hugged.

"Where have you been all night? We have been looking for you for hours! Are you all right?"

"Yes, yes, Dad, we're fine. If it wasn't for Mr. Frost and his kindness, I don't know what we would have done."

"Mr. Frost?"

"Yes, Mr. Frost and the beautiful little cottage deep in the woods." Mark pointed west into the woods.

"Boys, the old Frost cottage burned down twenty-five years ago!" Mark and Joel looked at each other in awe.

The Black Seal (cont.)

"No, Dad come and see!"

Mark grabbed his dad's hand and pulled him back up the trail they had just come down.

"Ok, boys. I know the way. I've never taken you there before because it is so deep into this forest."

Mark and Joel's dad moved down the trail until he found himself in the meadow where the boys had found Blaze. On the other side of the meadow, he took them into the woods. Soon they could see an old fireplace and chimney sticking up from the forest floor.

"This was the old Frost place," Dad said. "People say it was the most beautiful cottage in the area before it burned down. I think they called it, Dogwood Acres. Mr. Frost died in the fire. They say he was the nicest man in the county. He was full of love and kindness."

The boys could not believe what they were hearing and seeing! They knew they had spent the night here. They began running around the old chimney yelling, "We were here! We talked to Mr. Frost. He gave us skills to be better students in school and talked to us about being a winner! We sat right here!"

As Mark said that, he kicked a large burnt board over and saw a box. He bent down and grabbed a red cedar box from under the debris. "The box! Look, Joel!" On the top of the box were the words, **"SURVIVAL KIT."** Mark opened the box and in it was the parchment with the Pledge and the eight magic letters!

End of session #10

GRADES 4-5 LEADER'S GUIDE (CONT.)

Lesson 10 Questions
- What did you think of the ending?
- Where did the boys spend the night?
- What do you think they learned during this adventure?
- What does healthy positive attitude mean to you?
- What do you think the message of the story is?
- Would you like our class to start a Super Student Club and use the skills in this story?

Teacher

Super Student Skill Sheet #8
I WILL HAVE A POSITIVE, HEALTHY ATTITUDE.

Have your students work on this later in the day. After the worksheet is finished and shared, send these worksheets home to be signed. When they return, you can save these worksheets (there are eight of them) in a personal Super Student folder that at the end of the story will go home with the Super Student membership card and certificate.

The Super Student Pledge Word Find

Have your students use the Pledge Word Find (see the Black line masters). This activity is simple but fun and a good test for your students to learn the Pledge. Have the students check the word find against their copy of the Pledge.

The Super Student Focus Skills Checklist
(Highly recommended)

Have your students use this checklist at least twice a week to keep tabs on their attitude and behavior. This checklist is very useful for arrangements that you have with parents on daily reports that need to go home concerning the student's behavior.

Reasons Why

This is a survey to use only with those students who are on the edge of becoming a member of the club but you can tell that they are still not in the Super Student frame of mind. This is a highly confrontational survey so let the student take it and hand it in privately. You should only talk with the student in private if they hand it in to you in good faith.

Optional Activity

© Youthlight, Inc.

GRADES 4-5 LEADER'S GUIDE (CONT.)

8 Steps to Keep Your Attitude Positive

This is good to read together after your students have read this quietly. Conduct a good discussion on each of the steps and try to get the students to give you examples of people in their own lives who demonstrate these steps.

Teacher Hints

You will need to reinforce the Focus Skills and the Super Student Pledge each week in community circle by going over the skills and having your children memorize the Pledge. Keep them displayed in the room. By fourth and fifth grade they can read the Focus Skills and Pledge for themselves. Send home the prepared letter to the parents. With their parent's help, they can memorize the Focus Skills and the Pledge. I highly recommended that they do. Point out during the week who is doing which skill and how happy you are about the club.

Keep your club going all year long! It is very important to celebrate students and their efforts and achievements. Start today and make a big deal out of being a Super Student!

Counselors

This program allows you to involve a whole school for celebrating excellence and achievement grade by grade. Research has proven that effective schools focus on student effort and recognition of achievements (Marzano, 2001).

As you spearhead the Super Student Program and direct the Celebration Program that you should have at the end of every marking period, you will be creating a major impact on your school that is measurable and effective. It will fit into any goals based guidance program for the elementary schools. You will be creating a major positive change in your school as you start to celebrate your students based on the Super Student concepts. If you have the use of a TV studio in your school, your follow up in class and by TV will be very supportive for your teachers

THE SUPER STUDENT CLUB PACKET FOR GRADES 4-5

A tool is only good if you use it. The Super Student Program will only help you in the classroom if you use the concepts and skills. It is a tool, a survival kit, for you and your children. As you refer to the skills when you see them being used by your children, the students will respond and work harder for you. They will become the Super Students that you want. Be patient and persistent. After a while, these skills will become a habit and a way for your students to be successful in school. It will serve them not only with you this year but in future grades. In addition, it will become something that they will use as they progress into the world of work.

After the student signs the commitment sheet, his/her packet includes; the Super Student Focus Skills sheet, the pledge, membership card and certificate. Many teachers place the Super Student Focus Skills sheet and My Pledge right on the student's desk or on a bulletin board with each child's membership cards. Keeping the Super Student Focus Skills nearby allows you to visit the concepts during the day, if needed.

Teachers, many times, will take pictures with the students holding the membership cards. They will display the pictures where all visitors can see them. Teachers, send home the parent letters (see the Black line masters). In any case, it is important to display and continue to work with the concepts and skills during the community circle or group time throughout the year.

If you start the program at the beginning of the school year, I suggest that you have a mid-year contest for memorizing the Super Student Focus Skills and My Pledge. Enclosed in the Black line masters is a sample letter to the parents for this memorization challenge.

The more you celebrate your Super Students and draw attention to the Focus Skills and the Super Student Club the more your students will improve their Super Student behavior. I cannot stress this vital repetition to develop the skills so that they are habitual. Young children love this repetition. Please use any of the worksheet exercises in the Black line masters to bring your students the needed reminder of using the skills on a daily basis.

The parent information should go home. You will need to continue to secure the parent's cooperation for the program throughout the year. Remember to celebrate the winners of the club at each report card time. These are students who are using most of the skills on a regular basis. Look at the skills with them. Are they listening, raising their hand, being prepared for their work, giving their best, finishing their work, working out problems with others, and producing a positive healthy attitude in class? If so, they need to be celebrated.

Our school calls this a Renaissance Celebration, and we do it four times a year school-wide. I cannot stress using this celebration and recognition enough. It is vital that your school celebrates at least four times a year the product you are producing, namely students.

If your school has not adopted the Super Student Program school-wide, you can do this celebration in your classroom after report cards are given out. Invite the parents of the winners to the celebration. Encourage picture taking and serve refreshments. Celebrate your students!

★ SUPER STUDENT CLUB MEMBERSHIP

Dear Parents of Second through Fifth Grade Students,

We are beginning a special program, called the Super Student Club, at our school. This program will reinforce our instruction and achievement on a daily basis.

We need your help!
The Super Student Club was developed to help students:
- Take responsibility for their learning.
- Learn a systemic model for improving their schoolwork.
- Improve their effort toward academic tasks.
- Absorb basic study skills and concepts that improve the effectiveness and efficiency of their learning.
- Enhance self-esteem.
- Develop lifelong learners with positive healthy attitudes.

How can you help?
Please go over the Focus Skills and My Pledge with your child. He/she will have to learn and do these skills every day. Please support your child's teacher and sign this permission slip so they can join the Super Student Club. We believe that any student can be a Super Student. It is all about a super attitude! Please call us at the school if you have any questions.

★ Super Student Focus Skills

1. I will listen, obey, and trust my teacher.
2. I will raise my hand to speak.
3. I will think along with the speaker.
4. I will be prepared for my work.
5. I will give my best.
6. I will finish all my work.
7. I will work out problems with others.
8. I will have a positive, healthy attitude.

★ My Pledge

My attitude is the only thing I can control in life. I can choose to be happy or sad, helpful or hurtful. I can choose to be a winner in school. My attitude is reflected in these Super Student FOCUS Skills. I will read these Focus Skills every day. I will practice these skills to show I am a winner. People will see me doing these skills and good things will happen to me! As I focus on these skills, I will feel happy inside. Being GOOD is good for me! I really want to be a winner in school.

I give permission for my child to be in the Super Student Club. I will support the program. I will go over the Focus Skills and My Pledge with my child and keep in touch with his/her teacher throughout the year.

Child's name_____

Teacher_____ Grade_____

Parent Signature_____

ARE YOU A SUPER STUDENT?

Have you ever wondered if you are a Super Student?
Here is a quick way to tell if you are or might be. Read each question and answer Y for yes and N for no. When you are through, give this handout to your teacher. Be honest! Your answers will be kept private.

1. Do you almost always listen, obey, and trust your teacher?   Y   N
2. Do you raise your hand to speak in a group?   Y   N
3. Do you usually think along with the speaker when you are in class?   Y   N
4. Are you prepared for your work each and every day?   Y   N
5. Do you really give your best every day?   Y   N
6. Do you finish your work on time every day?   Y   N
7. Do you work out problems with others in a peaceful manner?   Y   N
8. Do you have a positive, healthy attitude?   Y   N
9. Are you respectful to your teachers?   Y   N
10. Are you respectful to your classmates?   Y   N

Count your yes and no answers.   **Total** ____Yes ____No

Write some questions for your teacher here about being a better student.

The Super Student Crossword Puzzle
THE OLD MAN

ACROSS

1. I must always try to do the _____ I can.
2. I am in control of my own _____.
3. Mark and Joel built themselves a _____ in the woods.
4. We learn when we listen to the _____.
6. The roof of the fort was made of _____.
9. While in school, my job is to be a Super _____.
11. It was Blaze's _____ to find birds in the woods.
12. I will _____, obey, and trust my teacher.
14. I am _____ for what I do and say.

DOWN

1. Mr. Frost gave the boys a _____ to keep them warm.
3. The boys lived in the middle of a huge _____.
5. I should come to school _____ to learn.
7. Mark and Joel's mom would always say, "It was not an _____ that things happened.
8. To be a Super Student you must have _____ in your life.
10. To be a good listener, I must _____ along with the speaker.
13. I want people who love and care for me to be _____ of me.

SUPER STUDENT SURVEY

Read each question and answer it as honestly as possible.

Today's date _____

Name _____ Grade _____

1. Are there many times that you refused to obey your teacher?   Yes   No
   If yes, why are you fighting inside when it comes to listening and obeying your teacher?
   _____
   _____

2. Do you call out in class without raising your hand?   Yes   No
   If yes, why do you call out? _____
   _____

3. If your classmates are answering and asking questions in class, do you ignore their comments?   Yes   No
   If yes, why do you ignore their comments? _____
   _____

4. Are you prepared for your work?   Yes   No
   If no, why are you not prepared? _____
   _____

5. Do you find yourself not giving your best many times in class?   Yes   No
   If yes, why? _____
   _____

6. Do you finish your work for class?   Yes   No
   If no, why are you not finishing your work? _____
   _____

7. Do you have problems working out bad feeling with other students?   Yes   No
   If yes, why are you unable to work problems out? _____
   _____

The Super Student Skill Sheet
THE OLD MAN

Skill #1

I WILL LISTEN, OBEY, AND TRUST MY TEACHER.

Super Student _____ Grade _____ Teacher _____

☺ Every time I listen, obey, and trust my teacher today, I will place a SMALL smiley face under the correct column.

LISTEN	**OBEY**	**TRUST**

TOTALS _____   _____   _____

Describe two of the times that you listened to your teacher today.

1.

2.

Describe two of the times that you obeyed and trusted your teacher today.

1.

2.

Parents/Guardian signature_____

THINK LIKE A WINNER! ACT LIKE A WINNER! BE A WINNER!

© Youthlight, Inc.

THE SUPER FORMULA

S **stands for SELF.** You must decide for yourself to become a Super Student. No one can do this for you. You can do it for your parents, relatives, teachers, or friends, but the decision to become a good student is yours alone. Nobody can make you a great student. The magic lies within you.

U **stands for UNDERSTAND.** You must understand the consequences of not doing well in school. You are throwing away time and possibilities when you are not becoming all that you can be. You can't make up time. We are all given just twenty-four hours a day, seven days a week. Once this time is gone, you will not get more. If you are wasting your years in elementary school, how will you get them back?

P **stands for PERSONAL.** Deciding to become a Super Student is a personal decision. Your mom or dad can't make it for you. Your attitude is the only thing you can control in life. It is a personal decision you make about how you will conduct each day of your life. If you make a personal decision to follow the Super Student Focus Skills, good things will happen to you.

E **stands for EFFORT.** Your effort counts! The more you try to become a SUPER STUDENT the more you will succeed! When you are working hard it becomes evident to you and all who are around you. ATTITUDE + EFFORT = RESULTS

R **stands for RESULTS.** You will become a SUPER student when you are focusing on the correct skills and the giving the required effort. You will then get the results that you want! Working hard, learning, achieving, acquiring good grades, and becoming happy about yourself as a student are goals you can achieve.

SUPER STUDENT DEFINITIONS: LISTEN, OBEY & TRUST

Our first Super Student Skill is, "I will listen, obey and trust my teacher." For some students this is difficult. Let's look at this important skill.

1. How are these three words different from each other?
   _____
   _____
   _____

2. How do they build on each other?
   _____
   _____
   _____

3. What does it take to obey your teacher? What part of yourself do you have to give up? _____
   _____
   _____

4. What is trust all about? _____
   _____
   _____

5. Who are some of the people that you trust in your life? Why do you trust them?
   _____
   _____
   _____

SUPER STUDENT DEFINITIONS: LISTEN, OBEY & TRUST

(Continued)

6. Why should you adopt your teacher as your best friend?
_____
_____
_____

7. What do you have to do to make that friendship work?
_____
_____
_____

8. Even if you do not like your teacher, why is it important to listen, obey, and trust him/her?
_____
_____
_____

9. Do you listen, obey, and trust your parents or guardians? Why or why not?
_____
_____
_____

10. Should you give your teachers the same respect that you give your parents or guardians? Why or why not?
_____
_____
_____

The Super Student Skill Sheet
THE OLD MAN

Skill #2
I WILL RAISE MY HAND TO SPEAK.

Super Student _____ Grade _____ Teacher _____

✓ Put a check mark every time you raise your hand to answer or ask a question during morning classes.

MORNING CLASSES

Total number of checks _____

Congratulations! Can you make this into a good habit?

Why should we raise our hands in class?

Why is asking a question just as important as answering a question?

What do manners have to do with raising your hand in class?

Parents/Guardian signature_____

THINK LIKE A WINNER! ACT LIKE A WINNER! BE A WINNER!

Try thinking of your teacher like this:
THE SUPER STUDENT WAY

1. Winners in school look at school as a way of improving and growing. School is a door that opens possibilities for you in life.

2. Teachers are the gatekeepers to this door. They are very important because they have something that you don't. They have knowledge. You are there to receive this knowledge.

3. You can only get this knowledge if you cooperate, work hard and learn to be obedient and trusting. If you trust them they will lead you in the right direction.

4. You need the teachers more than they need you. Do what the teachers ask and do it to the best of your ability. Things will work out for you.

5. Without the teacher's approval, all that you do will not benefit you. You must learn to work in the system to get the best the system has to offer.

6. Teachers place a lot of importance on the Super Student Focus Skills. Use them and you will be rewarded twice. Once from the teacher, and once for everything that you will learn.

7. You will meet many different kinds of teachers. Some you will like more than others. They are all adults who deserve respect because you are in a place where you can learn from them.

8. Don't worry all the time about how much you like the teacher. Continue to use the Super Student Focus Skills. These skills will see you through.

9. You show disrespect to yourself and your family when you disobey and disrespect your teacher.

10. Try looking at all the work the teacher is giving you as gold. The more you get the richer you are.

11. When the work gets hard, don't let the work beat you down. You beat the work!

12. If you think school is hard, try living in this world without an education!

Asking and Answering Questions...
CHECK IT OUT!

Student Activity 3.7

Super Student _____   Date _____

Teacher _____   Grade _____

Raising your hand in class is very important. You can raise your hand to ask or answer a question. What do you think is more imoortant?

Put a ✔ down for each time you raise your hand to ask or answer a question.

CLASS	ASKING QUESTION	ANSWERING QUESTION
1.		
2.		
3.		
4.		
5.		
6.		
7.		

TOTALS: ASKING _____   ANSWERING _____

The Super Student Skill Sheet
THE OLD MAN

Skill #3
I WILL THINK ALONG WITH THE SPEAKER.

Super Student _____ Grade _____ Teacher _____

Pick a class today and see if you are thinking with the speaker (Teacher and other students). Then, fill this out:

My teacher was talking about...

My body language was...

I know I was an active listener because...

One of the best questions I asked or answered was...

My eyes were always on the speaker.   ❑ YES   ❑ NO

Parents/Guardian signature_____

THINK LIKE A WINNER! ACT LIKE A WINNER! BE A WINNER!

The Super Student Skill Sheet
THE OLD MAN

Skill #4
I WILL BE PREPARED FOR MY WORK.

Super Student _____ Grade _____ Teacher _____

List the Super Student tools you have in your desk or cubby that you need to do your day's work: _____
_____

1. Being prepared with my tools today is important because:

2. Compare being prepared at school with a carpenter preparing to build a house. What does he need to do the job? Why?

3. How is school like a job?

4. I promise to be prepared every day because I am a Super Student.

Signed _____

Parents/Guardian signature _____

THINK LIKE A WINNER! ACT LIKE A WINNER! BE A WINNER!

© Youthlight, Inc.

The Top Ten Facts About Being
A SUPER STUDENT

1. **ANYONE CAN BE A SUPER STUDENT!**
   If you have a positive, healthy attitude, you can be a Super Student. It is all about a Super Attitude. You do not need to be born in a rich or special family. You will need to learn the skills that all good students use to produce winning habits that will allow you to be a winner in school.

2. **SUPER STUDENTS USE THE FOCUS SKILLS IN A HABITUAL WAY.**
   Good students have learned that the more that they use the Focus Skills the more the skills become a good habit. Teachers reward students when they use these skills over and over in class. These students are noticed in a good way that keeps the teacher thinking about them in a good way.

3. **SUPER STUDENTS ARE WINNING IN SCHOOL.**
   Because good students are using skills that work, they feel that they are on top or winning in school. They feel that they belong to a special club that is respected. After all, school is about learning and they have the special membership card to the club.

4. **SUPER STUDENTS ARE MADE NOT BORN.**
   Good students come from all kinds of backgrounds, races, economic, and cultural groups. Being a good student is about a super attitude not super ability. You do not have to be the best in everything. You only need to have one of the best attitudes.

5. **SUPER STUDENTS ARE HAPPIER THAN OTHER STUDENTS.**
   What a great feeling to know that you are in control of your behavior, actions, studies and school success! You are building for your future. Having a positive, healthy attitude promotes happiness. Want to be happy? Work on your attitude and learn the Focus Skills in the Super Student Program!

6. **SUPER STUDENTS APPRICIATE THE OPPORTUNITIES IN SCHOOL.**
   School is an opportunity to grow and develop your skills and strengths. Good students value the time they have when they are in school to grow. They know there will be a time that they will not have all day long to get instruction.

(Continued)

7. SUPER STUDENTS ARE THANKFUL.
America is a blessed country. We have a wonderful educational system and educational opportunities that is only dreamt about in other lands. Good students have a sense of thankfulness and take advantage of these opportunities that poor students are willing to throw away. This is one reason why students from other countries many times excel here.

8. SUPER STUDENTS ARE NOT AFRAID OF HARD WORK.
Good students know that anything worthwhile comes because of hard work. They are not afraid of challenging situations. They have learned that effort pays off. They are not quitters when the going gets tough. They know if they are lazy or will not apply themselves they will never be successful in anything they do. Don't look for the easy way. It doesn't exist!

9. SUPER STUDENTS ARE HELPFUL TO OTHER STUDENTS.
Good students have learned that they need others to help them be successful. They return this favor by helping others to be successful. Good students are not selfish with their learning. They have learned that their teachers have given to them. They need to return the favor to others.

10. SUPER STUDENTS ARE RESPECTFUL.
Great students always have a great sense of thankfulness and respect for their teachers and learning. They have learned that knowledge is a gift from teacher to student. It is passed along, not to be wasted. They know that without a teacher it is very difficult to learn something. We need each other as we grow. We need to share what we know with others. Super Students value learning highly.

SUPER STUDENT TO DO LIST

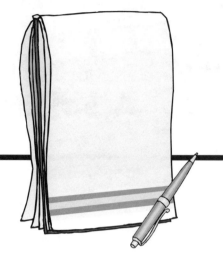

Things to do today:

✓ Make a list of what you need to do today! Be prepared for your work. Put a check in the box beside the task when you finish.

☐ 1._____
☐ 2._____
☐ 3._____
☐ 4._____
☐ 5._____
☐ 6._____
☐ 7._____
☐ 8._____
☐ 9._____
☐ 10._____
☐ 11._____
☐ 12._____
☐ 13._____
☐ 14._____
☐ 15._____

DID YOU GET IT ALL DONE? ☐ Yes ☐ No

The Super Student Skill Sheet
THE OLD MAN

Skill #5
I WILL GIVE MY BEST.

Super Student _____ Grade _____ Teacher _____

1. Describe one of the times today that you gave your best.

2. What does 'giving your best mean'?

3. Why is it important?

4. Write something nice to your teacher on the back of this work sheet. Read it to him/her.

Parents/Guardian signature_____

THINK LIKE A WINNER! ACT LIKE A WINNER! BE A WINNER!

12 TIPS FOR RAISING YOUR GRADES

1. **OBEY.** You will have many people who will be your boss. Learning to obey people who are in authority over you is very important in school and in life.

2. **RAISE YOUR HAND.** Raising your hand to ask and answer questions helps the teacher know you are listening and trying to learn.

3. **THINK ALONG WITH THE SPEAKER.** When you are in class you can learn a tremendous amount from your classmates when they speak.

4. **BE A GOOD LISTENER.** Look at people while they're talking to you. Pay attention to what they say. Repeat what they say quietly in your mind.

5. **WATCH YOUR BODY LANGUAGE!** Your eyes and the way you hold your body give your feelings away. Sit up and show respect when someone is talking to you in class.

6. **BE PREPARED.** You can't work if you do not have the tools to finish the job. Being prepared shows that you care. Have all your materials.

7. **GIVE YOUR BEST!** Effort is very important to your teacher and to success in school. The harder you try, the more likely you are to succeed.

8. **WATCH YOUR BEHAVIOR WITH OTHERS.** You must be able to work out problems with others. Fighting or arguing in school will hurt you as a student.

9. **PROJECT A POSITIVE ATTITUDE.** People like to be around a person who is upbeat and happy. Count your blessings. It will make you happy.

10. **LEARN TO TAKE NOTES.** One of the best tools you can have is learning how to take notes as your teacher speaks. It will help with your outlining and thinking skills.

11. **STUDY AT HOME ON A REGULAR BASIS.** You learn best in small repetitive ways. Going over your work every night in short sessions is best.

12. **FIGHT BEING LAZY!** All of us would rather play than work. Make yourself work first, play second.

The Super Student Skill Sheet
THE OLD MAN

Skill #6
I WILL FINISH ALL MY WORK.

Super Student _____ Grade _____ Teacher _____

Put a smiley face in each section where you finished all your work.

	Monday	Tuesday	Wednesday	Thursday	Friday
AM					
PM					

Questions:

1. What does 'beat the work mean'?

2. What should you do if you are having a problem with the work?

3. What does the way you finish your homework say about your character?

4. Why do you think that someone who finishes his/her work would be a good person to hire for a job? *(Please use the back to answer)*

Parents/Guardian signature_____

THINK LIKE A WINNER! ACT LIKE A WINNER! BE A WINNER!

© Youthlight, Inc.

SUPER STUDENT WEEK IN REVIEW

Student Activity 3.12

Today's date _____

Your Name _____

Think back on the week in this classroom. Read each statement, and then check the column that best describes how you feel about your behavior in school.

THIS WEEK IN SCHOOL	All of the time	Most of the time	Some of the time	Never
1. I respected my teacher.				
2. I obeyed my teacher.				
3. I trusted my teacher.				
4. I listened to my teacher.				
5. I raised my hand to answer questions.				
6. I was respectful to others.				
7. I treated others with respect.				
8. I helped others.				
9. I was prepared for my work.				
10. I gave my best in class.				
11. I finished my work.				
12. I worked out problems with others.				
13. I had a positive, healthy attitude.				
14. I felt accepted.				
15. I felt appreciated.				

© Youthlight, Inc.

Student Activity 3.13

BEATING THE WORK

**Finishing all your work is very important in school!
CONGRATULATIONS to you when you BEAT THE WORK!**

Super Student _____ Grade _____ Teacher _____

Color the magic seals when you finish your work in these subject areas.

MATH **READING** **SPELLING**

ENGLISH **SCIENCE** **SOCIAL STUDIES**

Total number of colored magic seals: _____   *Great Work!*

© Youthlight, Inc.

The Super Student Skill Sheet
THE OLD MAN

Skill #7

I WILL WORKOUT PROBLEMS WITH OTHERS.

Super Student _____ Grade _____ Teacher _____

Today Is: _____

☺ Every time I work out a problem with others, I will place a smiley face here and write a short note telling about what happened. I can talk it out, work it out, and move it out!

My Day:

Questions:

1. Why can problems with others ruin Super Students?

2. What are some of the tricks you can use if someone continues to bother you?

Parents/Guardian signature_____

THINK LIKE A WINNER! ACT LIKE A WINNER! BE A WINNER!

WORKING OUT PROBLEMS WITH OTHERS

When problems occur, and they will, here are some things you can do. Try it out!

1. WALK IT OUT!
Take a deep breath and cool down. When things get bad between you and another student, walk away and cool down before you speak or act.

2. FEEL IT OUT!
Describe your feelings raised by the conflict. Express yourself using respect as you talk to a trusted adult.

3. TALK IT OUT!
Go to an adult and talk it out. A teacher, counselor, principal or staff member at school is waiting to talk to you. They will help you to work it out.

4. WORK IT OUT!
Describe what is happening to a trusted adult who can help mediate. Try to look at both sides.

5. THINK IT OUT!
Brainstorm your problem with your trusted adult. Try to think of all the possible solutions to your conflict. Don't forget to come up with the possible outcomes to each solution.

6. TRY IT OUT!
See how one of your best solutions work. Give it your best. Tell your trusted adult how it is going. Don't stop your plan until you check in with your trusted adult!

7. STICK IT OUT!
Don't quit. Allow time for your plan to work. However, if you are threatened or feel afraid tell your trusted adult immediately!

Walk, Feel, Talk, Work, Think, Try, Stick it OUT!

© Youthlight, Inc.

SUPER STUDENTS USE "I MESSAGES"

"I messages" are great ways to get out of arguments with other students. It is a way to keep the conversation under control when you are in a conflict. Adults who deal with problems or problem people use this trick all the time. **Want to learn the secret?**

1. **USE THE WORD "I"** When your are dealing with a student who is bothering you, always begin your sentence with "I" not "You." "I" puts you in the driver's seat when you are talking. When you use the word "You", you put the person on the defense.

2. **USE FEELING WORDS.** Talk about how you feel next. "I feel" _____. Or I'm_____.

3. **SAY WHAT IS BOTHERING YOU.** State what the person did or is not doing that bothers you. I feel _____ when you _____. I'm feeling _____ when you _____.

4. **USE THE WORD WHY.** Tell why …. Use the word "because." I feel _____ when you _____ because _____.

5. **USE WHAT YOU WANT.** Then explain what you want. I want you to _____. OR I need you to _____.

Put the number of the rule for "I" messages on top of the words in each sentence. Examples:

1. I feel you are not being fair to me because I am not getting my turn to play. I need you to be fair.

2. I feel that you are being mean to me because of what you are saying. I need you to be nicer.

3. I feel that you are being hard on me for no reason that I can see.

4. I want you to be nicer to me. I feel that you are upset with me for some reason.

5. I want you to consider what you are asking me to do. I feel you are not considering my feelings.

The Super Student Skill Sheet
THE OLD MAN

Skill #8
I WILL HAVE A POSITIVE ATTITUDE.

Super Student _____ Grade _____ Teacher _____

I am most thankful for these things:

1. _____ 4. _____
2. _____ 5. _____
3. _____ 6. _____

These people have a positive healthy attitude:	How I know they do:
1. _____	_____
2. _____	_____
3. _____	_____
4. _____	_____

Write a short letter to a child in the hospital who is sick. Tell him/her why you are happy to be in your school and why you would like to invite them to your school when they are better.

Parents/Guardian signature_____

THINK LIKE A WINNER! ACT LIKE A WINNER! BE A WINNER!

TAKE THE PLEDGE!

My Pledge

My attitude is the only thing I can control in life. I can choose to be happy or sad, helpful or hurtful. I can choose to be a winner in school. My attitude is reflected in these Super Student FOCUS Skills. I will read these Focus Skills every day. I will practice these skills to show I am a winner. People will see me doing these skills and good things will happen to me! As I focus on these skills, I will feel happy inside. Being GOOD is good for me! I really want to be a winner in school.

I am signing this commitment sheet with my classmates and accepting my membership card for the Super Student Club. By signing this commitment sheet, I am saying that I want to be a Super Student and will use the Super Student Focus Skills everyday. My teacher has the right and responsibility to correct me when I stray from the Focus Skills and Pledge. I will also say the Pledge and abide by this Super Student Code. My teacher believes that I can be a Super Student. If I believe that I can, it will happen with hard work!

Signed:_____ Date: _____

Teacher_____ Grade _____

© Youthlight, Inc.

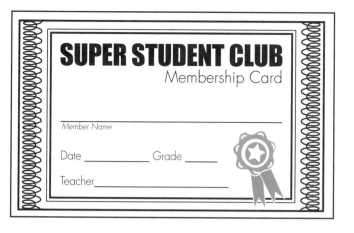

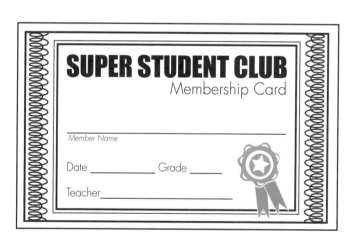

SUPER STUDENT
Certificate

This certifies that

_____

Has used the Focus Skills in class, has taken the Super Student Pledge, and is officially in the Super Student Club.

Teacher _____

Date _____

© Youthlight, Inc.

★ FOCUS SKILLS ★

1. I will listen, obey, and trust my teacher.
2. I will raise my hand to speak.
3. I will think along with the speaker.
4. I will be prepared for my work.
5. I will give my best.
6. I will finish all my work.
7. I will work out problems with others.
8. I will have a positive, healthy attitude.

My Pledge

My attitude is the only thing I can control in life. I can choose to be happy or sad, helpful or hurtful. I can choose to be a winner in school. My attitude is reflected in these Super Student FOCUS Skills. I will read these Focus Skills every day. I will practice these skills to show I am a winner. People will see me doing these skills and good things will happen to me! As I focus on these skills, I will feel happy inside. Being GOOD is good for me! I really want to be a winner in school.

THE SUPER STUDENT PLEDGE

Find the eight missing words in the pledge.

My Pledge

My _____ is the only thing I can control in life. I can _____ to be happy or sad, helpful or hurtful. I can _____ to be a _____ in school. My attitude is reflected in these Super Student FOCUS _____. I will _____ these Focus Skills every day. I will practice these skills to show I am a winner. People will see me doing these skills and _____ things will happen to me! As I focus on these skills, I will feel happy inside. Being GOOD is good for me! I really want to be a _____ in school.

SUPER STUDENT FOCUS SKILLS CHECKLIST

Are you doing these skills today?

Place a smiley face in front of each skill that you did all day long.

Today is _____

Super Student _____

Teacher _____ Grade _____

_____ I did listen, obey, and trust my teacher.

_____ I did raise my hand to speak.

_____ I did think along with the speaker.

_____ I was prepared for my work.

_____ I did give my best.

_____ I did finish all my work.

_____ I did work out problems with others.

_____ I did have a positive, healthy attitude.

How many smiley faces did you get today? _____

Teacher Comments:

Parent signature_____

Student Activity 3.18

Have you ever wondered why some students dislike school?
When we know the reasons for our behaviors, this can give us the power to change our behaviors.

Maybe one or more of these reasons are true for you. Read them, think about them, and then decide for yourself. Write answers only if you want to. Be honest.

1. What is the reason that you do not listen to your teacher?

2. Why don't you trust your teacher?

3. Why do you have a hard time obeying adults?

4. Why do you like to show off and try to get lots of attention?

5. Do you know why you do not raise your hand but just call out in class all the time?

6. When someone else is answering in class, do you know why you are not listening to what that person is saying?

7. Are you lazy? Why?

8. Why do kids pick on you at school and what do you normally do when they bother you?

9. Why do you have a hard time getting prepared for your work?

10. Why do you stop short of giving your best?

11. Why do you have a hard time finishing your work?

12. Why is it so hard for you to have a positive, healthy attitude?

13. Why do you act the way you do in school?

8 STEPS TO KEEP YOUR ATTITUDE POSITIVE

1. **Be Thankful.** People who have a positive, healthy attitude are thankful people. They are thankful for the things that people normally don't think about such as breathing, walking, running, seeing, and hearing. They look at the world differently. A flower or a sunset can turn their face into a smile. They are thankful that they are alive!

2. **Count your Blessings.** Is your cup half full or half empty? Super Students add up the good things that happen to them, not the bad. When you start counting the good things that are happening to you, your mind seems to be launching itself to better things. There is always someone in a situation that is worse than yours. Count your blessings.

3. **Tomorrow is another day.** Everyone has a bad day or a sad week once in a while. People who are positive are always willing to try again tomorrow. They may get down but they don't stay down. Winners in life are constantly pulling themselves up even though they get put down from time to time.

4. **Hang with people who are positive.** Have you heard that misery loves company? If you are always around people who are down or are always negative you will start finding yourself talking and acting like them. Positive people seek out people who will encourage them and drive them forward not backwards. If you are wondering why you are down all the time, what are your friends like?

5. **Use positive self-talk.** The human mind is a wonderful and awesome thing. It is a proven scientific fact that if you tell yourself something over and over your mind and body will start to believe it. Top athletes have known this trick for years. Talk to yourself in positive, uplifting ways throughout the day. Saying phases such as, "I am a good student, I can finish anything the teacher throws at me, I am strong and smart, I can be prepared for all my work, I can give my best, and I know I can work out any problem with my peers" is edifying. It works!

6. **Use visualization.** Again, whether from the sports world, business sector, or in humanitarian goals, winners in life visualize themselves winning and succeeding every day. Any goal that is set by the mind, if visualized, has a far greater chance of being met. See yourself winning in school in your mind's eye. Picture yourself listening in class, answering and asking questions, finishing work and scoring high on tests that you have prepared for. Positive people use visualization everyday to attain the goals they set for themselves.

7. **Turn lemons into lemonade.** The difference between a winner in school or life is the way you look at what is happening to you. Life will throw you lots of hurts as you continue to grow. Learn to change those lemon days into sweet lemonade. Positive people have the uncanny ability to change the bad that happens to them into good. Scott Hamilton, Olympic ice skating champion, had asthma as a child. He started ice-skating because it helped his breathing. As he continued to train, his asthma got better and better. History is full of people who, because of difficulties, became great.

8. **Lose that Pride.** One of the greatest obstacles to being a positive person and Super Student is your pride. Winners in life do not dwell on failures or setbacks. They are not afraid to ask for help and correction. They know that they are "under construction" and use every person or avenue to correct their course. If you are a person who always has to have it your way or can't be corrected, you are in for a bumpy road. When you give up your pride, you allow for millions of possibilities to get you back on the right track.

© Youthlight, Inc.

GOOD FOR YOU!

YOU GOT CAUGHT BEING GOOD.

_____ DID SOMETHING SPECIAL. You used these Super Student Focus Skills in class. Thank you for being a Super Student.

Date _____

✓ **Here are the Skills that you shared.**
(check all that apply)

_____ I did listen, obey, and trust my teacher.

_____ I did raise my hand to speak.

_____ I did think along with the speaker.

_____ I was prepared for my work.

_____ I did give my best.

_____ I did finish all my work.

_____ I did work out problems with others.

_____ I did have a positive, healthy attitude.

SUPER STUDENT FOCUS SKILLS & PLEDGE MEMORIZATION

Dear Parents of Second through Fifth Grade Students,

We need your help!
As you know, we have started the most important club your child can be part of at our school . . . The Super Student Club! This special program reinforces our instruction and achievement on a daily basis. The Super Student Club was developed so we could remind students daily about the skills that make winners in school. As you are aware, the Super Student Club has Focus Skills and My Pledge that we would like students to memorize. Could you please help your child learn all the skills and the pledge? We feel it is very important that the students learn the skills and make the pledge a part of their student life.

How can you help?
Please go over the Focus Skills and the Pledge with your child. He/she will have to learn and do these skills every day. Please support your child's teacher and sign this permission slip so they can join the Super Student Club. We believe that any student can be a Super Student. It is all about a super attitude! Please call us at the school if you have any questions.

★ **Super Student Focus Skills**

1. I will listen, obey, and trust my teacher.
2. I will raise my hand to speak.
3. I will think along with the speaker.
4. I will be prepared for my work.
5. I will give my best.
6. I will finish all my work.
7. I will work out problems with others.
8. I will have a positive, healthy attitude.

★ **My Pledge**
My attitude is the only thing I can control in life. I can choose to be happy or sad, helpful or hurtful. I can choose to be a winner in school. My attitude is reflected in these Super Student FOCUS Skills. I will read these Focus Skills every day. I will practice these skills to show I am a winner. People will see me doing these skills and good things will happen to me! As I focus on these skills, I will feel happy inside. Being GOOD is good for me! I really want to be a winner in school.

- -

RETURN TO TEACHER
I promise to teach the Super Student Focus Skills and My Pledge to my children and will see that he/she memorizes these important facts.

Student name_____

Teacher_____ Grade_____

Parent Signature_____

© Youthlight, Inc.

A SURVIVAL KIT
FOR THE TEACHER: *The Master Chef*

Eight Steps to Make the Super Student Magic Work!

Teachers need to know how to survive in today's schools. My heart goes out to today's educators who are working in classrooms across the nation. The stress and strain that they are experiencing now were unheard of thirty years ago. Pressure from within the system along with dealing with demanding parents and undisciplined children has made teaching a marathon race for most educators. It is not uncommon to hear teachers who have been teaching for two or three years asking about retirement or a job change.

The really successful teachers will relate to these suggestions about survival and focusing on elements that are the most important in successful teaching. It has been my experience that master teachers have learned to keep the world of teaching in perspective as they go about educating our youth. They do this by accepting the things they can and can't change. In addition, they have learned to focus on certain skills that allow them to produce great students.

Surviving, Thriving, and Enjoying the Ride

Because I have worked as a teacher and counselor for over 35 years and have had the good fortune to work with some of the finest master teachers in the country, I have come across some important concepts that have taught me how to survive in today's schools.

If you remember our short discussion earlier about thinking of your classroom as a gourmet kitchen, ready to make beautiful and delicious meals, you know that you can have the best ingredients and still not be able to produce a great meal because you do not possess the skills of a great chef. You must be able to do certain things in a skillful way to produce great results. It is the same in the classroom.

If you do not possess the necessary skills, you can't produce Super Students. It is my belief, one born out in research, that master teachers, like master chefs must have certain skills, or be willing to develop them in order to be effective with young people. If you do not have or want to develop these skills and attributes, please move out of education. You will do more damage than good, and you will not be happy. Educating young people is a wonderful but serious business. You are affecting children's lives for as long as they live.

Let's look at eight major gourmet techniques that master teachers embrace every moment that they are in front of their students. Use these with the Super Student Program and you will have little problem developing the students that you want. Plus, as a bonus, you will survive, thrive, and enjoy the ride!

The Magic 8
FOR TEACHERS

1. Be sincere and genuine in your love for children

These are perhaps the most important qualities you can have as an educator. Sincerity and being genuine can be developed. You must, however, have a sincere desire to change yourself. If you can ask yourself, "Do I really love children and believe that they can develop and change into people that are healthy and positive?" If you can answer this question with a yes, you are the right kind of person who will make a wonderful master teacher.

Sincerity is being honest with your feelings and being able to express them. As you love your students, tell them that you care and show them that love through the many acts of kindness that you do for them. Continue these feelings even during the tough times. Make sure that your love is not conditional or only valid if they are good.

Being genuine has to do with being the person you really are and not being afraid to become better. You can express your genuineness with your students by spending time with them and letting them know that the time you spend with them is important.

When you are doing any of your projects or lessons with your students, live in the moment. Project the feeling that whether you are involved in math, reading, science, or an art project with the class that you are making it the most important thing that you are doing at the moment. Let your class know that what the class is doing is wonderful, joyous, and very important to you.

When you can, make it a point to tell each individual privately that he/she is special. Please insure that each student feels your sincerity and genuineness in a special way. Their uniqueness will help guide you as you say uplifting things to each student in the class in your own personal way. Of course, some days you will just be happy to survive. We all have tough days and tough classes, but your daily attitude will be what influences your students the most.

What is love? One of the best definitions is found in the Bible. Paul in Chapter 13 of Corinthians gives us a clue. It suffers long and is kind. It shows no envy. It is not puffed up. It does not behave itself unseemly. It seeks not its own good. It is not easily provoked and thinks no evil. Love does not rejoice in evil but rejoices in the truth. It bears all things, believes all things, hopes all things, and endures all things. If you want a challenge, continue to grow in love with your students as it is described in Corinthians. It will not only develop them but it will have a profound effect on your life.

2. Be encouraging and passionate about teaching

I once heard a great definition of encouragement contrasting it with praise. Encouragement focuses on personal growth little by little as you progress and push yourself further and further. It can be given at anytime and does more to promote personal growth than anything known. It does not measure you against the group. It is not concerned with hitting a mark or goal. Encouragement is only concerned with per-

© Youthlight, Inc.

The Magic 8
FOR TEACHERS (Cont.)

sonal growth and development. Praise on the other hand is given only when you hit the mark, win the prize, or receive the award. As you can imagine, many students never get it!

The Super Student Program thrives on encouragement. Personal growth in any of the skill areas for each student is what slowly changes students who have bad habits or students who have no clue as to what makes a great student. Make encouraging statements to students such as, "John, you're raising your hand more than ever in the group, thank you!" Or "Jane, thank you for doing what I asked so quickly! I appreciate that!" When you do encourage them, you are encouraging future positive behavior and insuring that students will buy into the Super Student concepts and club.

Use encouragement every day in every class. Catch yourself building students up, instead of ripping and tearing them down. Students pick up on your tone of voice so be aware of how you are saying things. This can mean as much as **what** you are saying.

This does not mean, of course, that you will not correct students. Students need correction. It is part of 'being under construction.' The Super Student Program however encourages "catching students being good." When you find yourself encouraging your students throughout the day, you will see that they will give you what you want. How often and the manner in which you encourage, sets your relationship with your class and influences each individual in your class.

You are setting a positive tone when you are practicing sincerity, genuineness, love, and encouragement in your classroom. Students will pick up on these feelings.

If these important elements were the cars of a train, passion for teaching would be the engine that drives them. Passion is important in anything you do but is vital in teaching and influencing young people.

I am convinced that teachers have no idea of the amount of power and influence they have over children. They become so involved in the process and mechanics of teaching along with the preparation for lessons that they lose sight of the dynamics. They worry they are not reaching students but have little idea how much the students are listening, feeling and being influenced by the tone set in the classroom.

I have spent a lot of time with stressed teachers. They get down on themselves and it affects their teaching. You must be a cheerleader, even when the team is not doing that well. Tomorrow is another day and the students will pick up on your passion and optimism.

In short, don't expect students to be excited about anything you teach, including the Super Student Program if you are not excited about the subject! If you are not passionate about what you are doing, your students will pick up on these feelings and will not perform. They take their tone from you. You are vital in their development and growth.

You are on stage when you are working as a teacher. You can't let personal or private matters interfere with your daily work as an educator. So be on fire about what you are doing in the classroom. When you are in the classroom and on fire about your teaching, it is one of the most important things in the world! Guess what! It is.

3. Be knowledgeable in your subject area and make it relevant to students

One of the most obvious skills sometimes overlooked is how much you know about a subject that you are teaching. Master teachers know a lot about the areas that they are teaching. They are lifelong learners themselves. They travel, go to museums, art shows, sporting events, and music programs. They are interested in life and living and are usually exciting people to be around. They know how to fuse this excitement and the related facts into the lessons that they are teaching. They have healthy, positive attitudes.

Generally speaking, how can you teach something that you have not fully experienced or mastered? If you are a relatively new teacher, learn all you can about all the areas that you are teaching. If it's reading, are you an avid reader? If it is math, can you measure, build things, and make budgets balance? If it's writing, do you write stories, letters, use a diary or a journal? In other words, don't ask your students to do what you can't do or aren't willing to learn. Be a lifelong learner yourself! When you teach something, make it relevant to them. Use real life situations in your teaching as much as possible. 'Being there' experiences are the best way to immerse the children in the learning. So, run out there and experience this beautiful world and then share all that is good with your students. It will recharge you and motivate them.

I once had a math lesson that was a review of the basic operations with a group of fourth graders. We used their family grocery list to go mock shopping at a local grocery trying to find the best prices and best bargains. We then did the math to show their parents and guardians the best deals for them at the store and how to save money. Talk about relevant! I had little motivation problems with that lesson and was able to work it into science, language arts and art activities! Getting the parents involved made the unit very personal for each student. It was also interesting to see that I was getting more and more into the project as I saw the students turning on to what we were doing. It motivated me!

4. Be prepared for all lessons

You will have a lot fewer problems with discipline if you use the above suggestions and are fully prepared for each lesson. You must overplan for lessons and play the "what if game." Think about different scenarios that could take place during the lesson. Because of the problems with power or anger that some student have, you know what will happen as you start that special lesson that you have worked so hard to prepare. Plan with Murphy's Law in mind when you execute your lessons.

Be prepared with your plan using the Super Student concepts and make sure you have all your options in mind as you start the lesson. Being overplanned with your materials, lesson, or follow up is a great way to flow into lessons. You do not have to cover everything you planned but have these ideas and material ready to go as you need them. In other words, have additional plans in mind as the lesson unfolds. Then enjoy the ride!

5. Be respectful and allow student choice

When I was young and just starting in education, I worked with a teacher who told me that she didn't need to be respectful to her students. She told me that they were children and that she demanded their respect

The Magic 8 for Teachers (Cont.)

and should have it because she was the teacher! Well, it may sound good, but it doesn't work like that. By the way, she had all sorts of discipline problems especially with difficult students.

You have to earn your students' respect. It was true long ago and it still is today. Being respectful to your students will build your relationship and earn you the right to be respected. You will set the tone with your children as you work with them on a daily basis. They will imitate your manners in class. They will realize that they are valuable and start to believe it. They will also believe that you value them as people worthy of respect. When this happens you can teach them anything.

If you recall, one of the main concepts of the Super Student Program was that you believe that students can change and become better. As a student is treated with respect, and you show that you love and believe in that person, the possibilities that he/she will change increases. Please note that I say increases. It will never be 100 percent.

Children, like adults, make choices about their lives. You are not responsible for those choices, but you influence the atmosphere in which they are made. In other words, as a teacher or counselor you create the climate for the decision.

The suggestions thus far are meant to create the best conditions for the students that you have so that they make good, healthy, and responsible choices. In the end the student will choose. You must respect, but do not necessarily have to agree with, the choices they make.

The manner in which you respond to their choices is extremely important. Some teachers that I have worked with hold themselves responsible for the choices that students make. They go around saying to themselves, "Well, I'm sorry if I have to be so mean, but I need to teach these children to behave." Don't feel guilty! The student has put himself in the situation. Let him feel the full weight of the decision! It will help him/her to change. Continue to love and encourage that child and wait for the next opportunity.

I have learned through the years that protecting people from pain after they have made a bad choice is a mistake. Pain is of course not pleasant but is a wonderful teacher! It is difficult for some people to step back and say, "Well, if this is your choice, this will be the consequence of your decision and you will have to live with it. I care for you and love you. I want you to be happy, but if you do this, this is what will happen. It's your decision and I will respect it."

At this point you need to follow through with the consequences that are natural or logical. Let the student feel the weight of his/her decision. Of course, I am not talking about dangerous consequences that would endanger the child but normal and natural consequences that are the foundation of good discipline.

For example, I once had a student come to me and say, "Dr. Chanaca, the students are laughing at me when I suck my thumb in class! Can you help me?"

I guess he wanted me to talk to the whole class and have them stop the teasing. I asked him (he was a fifth grader), "What do you think you can do to stop the kids from teasing you?"

He replied, "I guess I could stop sucking my thumb in front of them."

"Good idea! Let's try it for three weeks and then come back to me and let me know how it is going." I gave him an appointment card and three weeks later he was happy to report that the teasing had stopped.

He felt that he had worked it out and owned the results of his decision. The truth is that people need to feel that they are responsible for their decisions. The fact that a student has chosen to be a Super Student is a personal decision. They will own their choices if they are allowed to make them and accept the consequences. It works like that in all decisions. This is what creates a responsible person. When students see that you hold them responsible for making decisions and they learn to accept the consequences of their decisions, they will own their own behavior. If a student chooses not to be a Super Student, honor their choice and let the door open for the student to come back. If it's not their choice, they will not own it, and it will not be something that lasts.

6. Be aware that change is difficult

Do you have things in your life that you would like to change? Do you have habits that continue to be in the way of your being the kind of person that you would like to be? So do your students.

When I think of some of the children that I have worked with over the years and the family situations that they came from, I am amazed at how well they are doing in school. I ask myself, "How would I have performed in that situation?" It is hard enough for a person in a loving family with their real mom and dad to overcome selfish desires, anger, jealously, and hatred. Can you imagine what it is like for Jimmy, whose father is dead because of a drug deal gone bad? How about Alice, whose mother is in prison because she shot her boyfriend who was abusing the older sister on a regular basis? Would you have done your homework if you were living with a grandmother who was sickly and a grandfather who was a drunk?

A student like Jimmy is coming to school to meet you. Do you think he/she may be angry? Do you think he/she wants to listen to you every time you ask him to do something? Maybe. If he does, you have a real gem in front of you.

Jimmy may want to change, but perhaps he doesn't have a clue where to start. He will need to find a person he can trust, love, and follow. I hope that person is you! He will then need a plan. That is where the Super Student Program fits into your plan. The Super Student concepts will give him the tools he needs to survive and grow.

Remember the movie "Antwone Fisher"? If you haven't seen it, check it out this week. It will make my point. You see children come with baggage that you might not know about. Find out. It's your job! Finding out where people are coming from is the mark of a great teacher. Realize what turns a person on. Then, take a deep breath, whisper a short prayer and dive in. It's called teaching!

7. Be patient

This has been a tough one for me. I am learning to be more patient every day. I still have a way to go. Although change is difficult, the teacher who can be longsuffering will allow love, in time, to work miracles. If you can project the image that you are 'sticking in there for as long as it takes,' most students will respond.

A person can get used to rejection and abuse over time. He/she gets callous and hard as concrete. However, water over time

The Magic 8 For Teachers (Cont.)

can wear away concrete. If you are longsuffering you will win children over. They will realize that you're not going away, and that you continue to say the same encouraging things. Your love is constant.

I know this is hard. Believe me! This is perhaps the single biggest reason we lose students even when we are doing everything right. We get tired! If you can be tougher than the student, you will both win.

8. Be optimistic and keep a sense of humor

It's teaching, not surgery! Believe me, you are going to have a lot of chances to make it right. Students that you are working with come from all kinds of backgrounds. You have a wonderful opportunity to influence them in so many positive, healthy ways. Be optimistic and believe that all the good you are doing is felt by your students and will be remembered.

I am constantly amazed by the students I have had. They remember lessons or situations that are long gone from my memory. They come up to me and say, " Hey, Dr. C, do you remember such and such? It meant so much to me!" I say, "Thank you so much for sharing that!" (even if I don't remember the incident.)

If your intentions are good and unselfish, you're not going to cause any harm. Give it a great try and let children know that we all make mistakes, and we are all in the process of growing. We're in this together. You're just asking to grow along with them for a while. Have fun while you do!

Laugh privately at some of the crazy things kids and parents do. I once had a kid who stuck his finger in the facet as he was trying to squirt girls with water! He cried. It took a plumber to remove it, but he didn't fool around like that again for the rest of the year.

Keep your sense of humor, or develop a better one. You will need it for your survival. Learn to laugh at yourself when you make a mistake. You need to laugh and it will refresh you! So, use humor and laughter generously. It's good for you!

A SURVIVAL KIT
FOR THE PARENT

No program in American education would be complete without parental involvement. Parents are vital as partners and need to feel and know that they are the major factor in helping their children be Super Students.

No one else has such a major impact on a child's life as you do. How can you help to develop your child into a lifelong learner? How do you lead your child to be a Super Student? We will look at how you can support the Super Student concepts and skills. Also, we will explore some great parenting skills that promote a positive and loving attitude that will make your child a winner in school and in life.

The Super Student Program and club was developed to help students:

- Learn a systematic model for improving their schoolwork.

- Improve effort toward academic tasks.

- Absorb basic study skills and concepts that improve the effectiveness and efficiency of their learning.

- Enhance self-esteem in the learning experience.

- Develop into lifelong learners with positive, healthy attitudes.

How can you help? Please go over the Super Student Focus Skills and My Pledge with your child. He/she will have to learn and do these skills every day. Please support your child's teacher by attending all conferences and meetings. Let your child know that you believe in the Focus Skills and Pledge and will back the teacher in implementing them in class. Believe that your child can become a Super Student! Then, tell them all the time. It is all about a Super attitude!

Please look at the Focus skills to be a Super Student:

1. I will listen, obey, and trust my teacher.

2. I will raise my hand to speak.

3. I will think along with the speaker.

4. I will be prepared for my work.

5. I will give my best.

6. I will finish all my work.

7. I will work out problems with others.

8. I will have a positive, healthy attitude.

Your child's teacher is working with these skills during community circle every day for the next ten weeks. Will you support him/her? Talk to your children about the stories and discussion the class is using as they study and learn these skills in order to be great students.

Call your child's teacher to let him/her know that you support their efforts to work with and develop your child's skills. Every other

© Youthlight, Inc.

A SURVIVAL KIT
FOR THE PARENT *(Cont.)*

day a new part of the Super Student story is introduced that will discuss one of the skills on the Super Student Focus Sheet.

Then, your child will be asked to join the Super Student Club that will last all year long. These Focus Skills will be taped on your child's desk or displayed on the wall in class for him/her to refer to during the day.

Please go over the pledge with your child. It would be a great advantage to have your child memorize it. We encourage it!

MY PLEDGE

My attitude is the only thing I can control in life. I can choose to be happy or sad, helpful or hurtful. I can choose to be a winner in school. My attitude is reflected in these Super Student Focus Skills. I will read these Focus Skills every day. I will practice these skills to show I am a winner. People will see me doing these things, and good things will happen to me! As I focus on these skills, I will feel happy inside. Being GOOD is good for me! I really want to be a winner in school!

Your child will also receive a Super Student Membership Card and Certificate. Ask your child about the card and certificate. In some schools, there may be a celebration or ceremony for the club. If you are invited, attend the celebration. All of this, along with your personal communication with your child's teacher, will build your child into the Super Student that you and the teacher want to have.

One of the major lessons you can teach your child is the first Focus Skill: to listen, obey and trust their teacher. Let your child know that you support the teacher and his/her authority. Not insisting on this is one of the major mistakes that parents make. When you undermine your child's teacher's authority you give your child permission to be disrespectful. You are setting the atmosphere for a major mistake that will pull your child down. If you disagree with a teacher, keep it private between you and the teacher. Don't discuss negatives about the teacher in front of your child.

Yes, you love your children! Giving them support during their school years is one of the greatest things you can do for them to show your love. They are only young once; this is your opportunity to develop them in a healthy way. As a bonus, you grow along the way!

Don't miss this opportunity! You are making an investment in your child's future. School is so important in today's world!

How can you help beyond the Super Student Program? Check out the eight major ideas to support your parenting.

The Magic 8 — For Parents

1. Be sincere and genuine in your love for your children.

These are perhaps the most important qualities you can have as a parent. Be aware that you have the awesome task of raising and nurturing a young life. You are responsible for another human being. Sincerity and genuineness can be developed. However, you must have a sincere desire to change yourself. If you can be in touch with yourself and ask, "Do I really love my child and believe that he/she can develop into someone that is healthy and positive?" If you can answer this question with a yes, you are the kind of person who will make a wonderful parent, even if you do not have a clue where to start.

Look at the sincerity of your heart. If you are honest about your parenting, you will find the way. Is there a more important thing that you can be doing with your life than loving and raising your child? I don't think so.

Sincerity is being honest with your feelings and being able to express them. As you love your child, tell him/her that you care and show them through many acts of kindness that you do. Let him/her know how you feel about them. If this were your last day on this earth, with whom would you spend it? What would you say to your children during the day? What would you do with them? Enjoy your parenting, and live each day as if it were your last day!

Being genuine has to do with being the person you really are and not being afraid to become better. You can express your genuineness with your children by spending time with them and letting them know that the time you spend with them is important. When you are doing any of your outings, projects, or lessons with them, live in the now. Project the feeling that whether you are involved in school work, outings, or private time that you are making it the most important thing that you are doing at the moment. Have fun with your kids!

When you can, make it a point to tell your child that he/she is special. Please see that your child feels this sincerity in a very special and individual way. Their uniqueness will help guide you as you say uplifting things to each of your children in your own personal way. Of course, there will be some days you will just be happy to survive. We all have tough days. But your attitude and love will be what your child feels and experiences. I guess what I am talking about is love.

What is love? Paul in Chapter 13 of Corinthians in the Bible gives us a clue. He says it suffers long and is kind. It shows no envy. It is not puffed up. It does not behave itself unseemly. It seeks not its own good. It is not easily provoked and thinks no evil. Love does not rejoice in evil, but rejoices in the truth. It bears all things, believes all things, hopes all things, and endures all things. If you want a challenge, continue to grow in love with your children. It will not only develop them, but it will have a profound effect on your life.

© Youthlight, Inc.

The Magic 8 for Parents (Cont.)

⭐ 2. Be encouraging and passionate about raising your children.

I once heard a great definition of encouragement contrasting it with praise. Encouragement focuses on personal growth little by little as you progress and push yourself further and further. It can be given at any time and does more to promote personal growth than anything known. It does not measure you against the group. It is not concerned with hitting a mark or goal. Encouragement is concerned with personal growth and development. Praise, on the other hand, is given only when you hit the mark, win the prize, or receive the award. Give huge amounts of encouragement to your children.

The Super Student Program thrives on encouragement and so does great parenting. Personal growth in any of the Super Student skill areas for each student is what slowly changes students who have bad habits or students with no clue how to be a great student. Make encouraging statements to your child such as, "I heard from your teacher that you're raising your hand more than ever in the group. Thank you!" Or "Jane, thank you for doing what I asked so quickly! I appreciate that!" When you do encourage them, you are encouraging future positive behavior and insuring that children will buy into the Super Student Club and your leadership at home.

Use encouragement every day at home. Catch yourself building your children up, instead of ripping and tearing them down. This does not mean, of course, that you will not correct your kids. Children need this correction. It is part of 'being under construction.' When you find yourself encouraging your children throughout the day, you will see that they will give you what you want. How often and the manner in which you do it, sets your relationship with your family.

You are setting a tone when you are dealing with sincerity, genuineness, love, and encouragement in your home. Children will pick up on these feelings and emotions or the lack of them. If these important elements: sincerity, genuineness, and encouragement, are the cars of a train then passion would be the engine that drives them.

Passion is important in anything you do, but it is vital in parenting and influencing young people. I am convinced that parents have no idea how much power and influence they have over their children. They become so involved in the process and mechanics of parenting, along with life's other duties, that they lose sight of the dynamics. Of course, there are parents who are so involved with their own lives that they have no idea how much they are destroying their families, and themselves in the process. Sometimes they worry they are not reaching their kids but they have little idea how much the kids are listening, feeling and experiencing.

I spend a lot of time with stressed parents who are not looking at the big picture. You must be a cheerleader, even when the team is not doing that well. Tomorrow is another day, and your children will pick up on your passion and optimism.

In short, don't expect your children to be excited about anything you teach, do, or share with them if you are only 'going through the motions.' If you are not passionate about what you are doing, your children will pick up on these feelings and will not perform. They take their tone from you. You are vital in their development and growth. So be on fire about what you are doing at home. Share it with them. When you are there, doing it with them, it is the most important thing in the world that is happening.

★ 3. Be involved in your children's schooling

School is major part of your child's life and development. If you think about it, formal schooling can start as early as four years of age. It continues well into adulthood. It is important because it prepares children for life and work. Also, this is what children do as their job.

Of course education is vital in today's world. Staying involved in it is critical to good parenting. Going to the school conferences, communicating with your child's current teacher, attending many of the school functions, and supporting all the programs that touch your child's life is essential. Checking your child's report cards and following up on your child's scores in the school's testing program is also part of good and effective parenting.

What do you think it tells your children if you do not attend a scheduled conference about them? It tells them that you have better things to do than to be involved in their school life. It tells them that you have your life to live, and you don't have time to bother yourself with their school life. Is it any wonder that we have so many upset students in school that aren't achieving? One of the major ways that we tell people that we love them is by being interested in what they are doing. Do you know what your child thinks of school, the teacher, or the kids in his/her class? Do you know how they are doing in their classes? What are their strengths and weaknesses? It's your job to find out.

© Youthlight, Inc.

The Magic 8 for Parents (Cont.)

4. Respect your children and allow choice to develop responsibility.

Do you respect your children? Do they respect you? You have to earn your child's respect. It was true long ago and it is still true today. Being respectful to your child will build your relationship and earn you the right to be respected. You will set the tone with your children as you work with them on a daily basis.

They will imitate your manners and attitude. They will realize that they are valuable. They will also believe that you value them as people. Let them know that they are fun to be with and that you could not live without them.

If you remember, one of the main concepts of the Super Student Program was that you must believe that children can change and become better. As a child is treated with respect and you show that you love and believe in that person, the possibilities that he/she will change increases. Note that I say, increases. It will never be 100 percent.

Children, just like adults, make choices about their lives. They will make millions of them in the course of their lives. You are not responsible for all those choices but you influence the atmosphere in which they are made. In other words, as a parent you create the climate for the decision. Your guidance with these decisions is what forms the child's responsibility they will take for the decisions. The freedom you give your children to make these decisions must be age appropriate of course. Allowing little children to make small decisions and reap the consequences is practice for the larger decisions that they will make as they are older.

The suggestions thus far are trying to create the best conditions for the child that you have so that they make good, healthy and responsible choices. In the end the child will choose. You must respect but do not necessarily have to agree with the choices they make.

The manner in which you respond to their choices is extremely important. Many parents that I have worked with hold themselves responsible for the choices that their children make. They go around saying to themselves, "Well I'm sorry if I have to be so mean but I need to show my kids how to behave!" They feel guilty. Don't feel guilty! The child has put himself in the situation. He needs to feel the full weight of his decision! It will help him/her to change. This is what natural and logical consequences are all about. Continue to love and encourage that child and wait for the next opportunity to continue to mold him/her.

I have learned through the years that protecting people from pain after they have made a bad choice is a mistake. A difficult situation is a wonderful teacher! It is difficult for some people to step back and say, "Well, if this is your choice, this will be the consequence of your decision and you will have to live with it. I care for you and love you. I want you to be happy but if you do this, this is what will happen. It's your decision and I will respect it!"

At this point you need to follow through with the consequences that are natural or logical.

Let your child feel the weight of his/her decision. Of course, I am not talking about dangerous or serious consequences that would endanger your child. You will need to make these decisions. There are, however, many age appropriate decisions that are great learning times for children. Use these times well and don't be too overprotective.

The truth is that people need to feel that they are responsible for their decisions. The fact that a child has chosen to be a Super Student is a personal decision. They will own their choices if they are allowed to make them and accept the consequences. It works like that in all decisions. This is what creates a responsible person. When children see that you hold them responsible for making decisions, and they learn to accept the consequences of that decision, they will own their own behavior.

5. Be aware that change is difficult

Do you have things in your life that you would like to change? Do you have habits that continue to be in the way of you being the person that you would like to be?

So do your children as they try to grow up in a difficult but wonderful world. You are competing with so many negative influences that touch your children's lives that you must be vigilant to screen and monitor all of your kids involvements and activities. These negative influences will slow positive changes down. Also, children, like adults, are constantly being pulled from the inside to take the easy way out. This is where your guidance and parenting must come into play. Let your kids know that you went through many of the same difficult decisions and trials that they are going through. Let them know that you will always be with them as they go through the difficult times and you will never desert them. And then, please, keep your promise!

The Magic 8 for Parents (Cont.)

⭐ 6. Be patient

This is a tough one for me. But I am learning. Although change is difficult, the parent who can be longsuffering will allow love, in time, to work miracles. If you can project the image that you are hanging in there for as long as it takes, children will respond. A person can get accustomed to rejection and abuse over time. He/ she gets callous and hard as concrete. However, water over time can wear away concrete. If you are longsuffering you will win your children over. They will realize that you're not going away and that you continue to say the same encouraging things. Also, you allow them to know that your love is longsuffering.

I know this is hard. Believe me! This is perhaps the single biggest reason we lose our children even when we are doing everything right. We get tired! If you can be tougher than your child and can see the future, you will both win.

⭐ 7. Be optimistic and keep a sense of humor

It's parenting, not surgery! Believe me, you are going to have a lot of chances to make it right. The children that God has given you are unique. You have a wonderful opportunity to influence them in so many positive, healthy ways. Be optimistic and believe that all the good you are doing is felt by your children and will be remembered by them.

I am constantly amazed by my own children's comments. They remember lessons or situations that are long gone from my memory. They come up to me and say, " Hey Dad, do you remember such and such. It meant so much to me!" I say, "Thank you so much for sharing that!"

If your intentions are good and unselfish, you're not going to mess anyone up. So, give it a great try and let your children know that we all make mistakes and we are all in the process of growing. We're in this together. You're just asking to grow along with them a while. Have fun while you do!

Laugh privately at some of the crazy things kids do. Once my son, Joel, who was learning how to ride a bicycle, started to pedal the bike down a steep hill. My wife, Jane, and I were yelling, "brakes, brakes!" Luckily, he made it to the bottom of the hill unharmed.

Keep your sense of humor or develop a better one. You will need it for your survival. Learn to laugh at yourself during the day. You need to laugh and it will refresh you! So, use laughter generously. It's good for you.

© Youthlight, Inc.

8. Be there and be forgiving

Children need to know constantly that you will be there and that you will forgive their mistakes as long as they are trying to make things right. One of the scary things about raising kids is that you will see yourself in them as you continue to watch them develop. I think it is God's little joke to keep us humble. There are things in your own life that you are not happy about and struggle with daily. Maybe it's temper, thoughtlessness, or selfishness. Whatever it is, your child will eventually catch it! You receive a personal second chance to try to work out the same problems through your children. So, you're both under construction in God's eyes. Be forgiving and continue to work on things in your own life as well as your children's lives.

ABOUT THE AUTHOR

Dr. John Chanaca has had over 35 years of teaching and counseling experience in the public schools of Pennsylvania and South Carolina. Currently, he is a counselor in Horry County Schools, South Carolina. After completing his Bachelors and Masters Degrees in elementary education, he taught in various elementary and middle schools at various locations with different social, economic and cultural groups. He obtained his certification in counseling from Marywood University in PA. For the past 19 years, he has practiced as a counselor in the public schools at various levels. For four of those years, John acted as the head of special education placements in his district. John also holds a certification in public school administration from Penn State University. In addition, he has been a Licensed Professional Counselor (LPC) since 1985 and has a private Christian Marriage and Family practice.

John received his Doctorate in Education from the University of South Carolina (1992) concentrating in curriculum and instruction. He has supervised over fifty student teachers and interns in both education and counseling. In addition, John has taught part time at several colleges and universities in both the education and counseling departments.

In October of 1998, Dr. Chanaca was selected as a Fulbright Memorial Fund Scholar to Japan to study their educational system. This trip inspired Dr. Chanaca to begin writing the Super Student Program.

He is a co-author of the AGS program, Peer Pals. This program has received several national and state awards. Peer Pals is a motivational program for elementary school students focusing on positive learning attitudes and self-esteem in a peer helping setting.

Dr. Chanaca is a third degree Black Belt in Tang Soo Do. During his presentations in motivational workshops and conferences across the United States, Dr. Chanaca combines his love of the martial arts with successful programs and strategies. These programs focus on positive life style techniques that benefit students, educators and parents.

For more information and inquiries for workshops on the Super Student Program or other motivational talks, e-mail Dr. Chanaca at jchanaca@aol.com or call 1-843-248-3401.

★ REFERENCES

Bowman, R. P. & Chanaca, J. (1994). *Peer Pals: Kids Helping Kids Succeed in School.* Circle Pines, Minnesota: American Guidance Service, Inc.

Cameron, J., & Pierce, W.D. (1994). Reinforcement, reward, and intrinsic motivation: A meta-analysis. Review of Educational Research, 64, 363-423.

Marzano, R. J. (1998a). *A theory-based meta-analysis of research on instruction.* Aurora, CO: Mid-continent Research for Education and Learning. (ERIC Document Reproduction Service No. ED 427 087).

Marzano, R. J. (1992). *A different kind of classroom: Teaching with dimensions of learning.* Alexandria, VA: Association for Supervision and Curriculum Development

Marzano, R. J. (2000a). *A new era of school reform: Going where the research takes us.* Aurora, CO: Mid-continent Research for Education and Learning. (ERIC Document Reproduction Service No. ED454255)

Marzano, R. J. (2003). *What works in schools, translating research into action.* Alexandria, VA: Association for Supervision and Curriculum.

Marzano, R. J., Gaddy, B.B. & Dean, C. (2000). *What works in classroom instruction?* Aurora, CO: Mid-continent Research for Education and Learning.

Marzano, R. J., Pickering, D. J. & Pollock, J. E. (2001). *Classroom instruction that works: Research-based strategies for increasing student achievement.* Alexandria, VA: Association for Supervision and Curriculum Development.

Marzano, R. J. Norford, J. S. , Paynter, D. E., Pickering, D. J. & Gaddy, B. B. (2001). *A Handbook for classroom instruction that works.* Alexandria, VA: Association for Supervision and Curriculum Development.

Seligman, M. E. P. (1990). *Learned optimism.* New York: Pocket Books.

Seigman, M. E. P. (1994). *What you can change and what you can't.* New York: Alfred A. Knopf.

Urdan, T., Midgley, C. & Anderman, E. M. (1998). The role of classroom goal structure in students' use of self-handicapping strategies. *American Educational Research Journal,* 101-122.

Van Overwalle, F., & DeMetsenaere, M. (1990). The effects of attribution-based intervention and study strategy training on academic achievement in college freshmen. *British Journal of Educational Psychology,* 299-311.

Wiersma,U. J. C. (1992). The effects of extrinsic reward on intrinsic motivation: *A meta-analysis Journal of Occupational and Organizational Psychology,* 101-114.

Wilson, T. D., & Linville, P. W. (1982). Improving the academic performance of college freshman: Attribution theory revisited. *Journal of Personal and Social Psychology,* 367-376.